Our Minnesota

REVISED THIRD EDITION

Photographs & Captions by
Les, Craig & Nadine Blacklock
Text by Fran Blacklock

VOYAGEUR PRESS

Revised Third Edition
ISBN 0-89658-221-3 (hardcover)
Text copyright 1992 by Fran Blacklock
Photographs and captions copyright 1992 by
Les, Craig, and Nadine Blacklock

First published by Voyageur Press, copyright 1978 by
Les and Fran Blacklock
Revised, expanded edition published by Voyageur Press, copyright 1981 by
Les, Fran, and Craig Blacklock

Printed in Hong Kong
92 93 94 95 96 5 4 3 2 1

Library of Congress Cataloging-in-Publication Data available

Published by
VOYAGEUR PRESS, INC.
P.O. Box 338, 123 North Second Street
Stillwater, MN 55082 U.S.A.
From Minnesota and Canada 612-430-2210
Toll-free 800-888-9653

Voyageur Press books are also available at discounts for quantities for
educational, fundraising, premium, or sales-promotion use. For details
contact the marketing department. Please write or call for our free catalog of
natural history publications.

Contents

Introduction

Les and I once had an assignment to cover the entire state of Minnesota, recording in words and pictures the many things of interest there are to see and do. Our work was published by the then Department of Business Development in booklets featuring six regions of the state, the first in a number of series put out by the state. Over time, for the Minnesota Office of Tourism and for *Our Minnesota,* the six regions have been redrawn as four: the Metro, the Northeast, the Northcentral/West, and the South.

It was a wonderful experience for us to learn to know Minnesota and her people in every nook and cranny. From sunup until after dark each day, we journeyed from town to town traveling more than seven thousand miles, talking with people, and learning about places of scenic beauty or special interest.

Along with feasting our eyes on the scenery, we marveled at the people. In visiting hundreds of tourist attractions, shops, museums, and resorts, we never met any who were not genuinely interested in telling us about their places and about a personal hobby such as collecting or skills such as wood carving, taxidermy, and potting.

Knowing about the past, about the land, about the people who first came and what they did, can add to your enjoyment while traveling through Minnesota.

This book is not meant to be a travel guide, but it points out some places that Les and I have found to be of special interest through our own experiences. In this brief account, many places are omitted, but that leaves exploring and discovery for you to do, and that's a good part of the fun. Get off the highways. Do a little research ahead of time. And enjoy!

Regions of Minnesota

Canoe at portage in BWCAW. —L.B.

We Chose Minnesota

Les and I have had an incurable love affair with Minnesota for many years now. While we were growing up, he in Moose Lake and I in Minneapolis, we took Minnesota more or less for granted. We were born here, and there was no thought on our part or that of our parents of living anywhere else. As adults we have chosen to live in Minnesota.

This is a stimulating state to live in. Its variety spices up things considerably. The southeastern corner fringed with the bluffs of the winding Mississippi River contrasts with the flat tabletop fields of the northwestern section of the state. The northeastern or Arrowhead region, with its expansive forests and rock-shored lakes and rimmed by the North Shore of Lake Superior, is rugged country, quite unlike the gentle lake lands of central Minnesota or the rolling farmlands of the southwest.

Our climate affords variety, too, making the "weather news" one of the most popular and necessary offerings on television and radio. In winter when the snow falls, it stays, accumulating for good skiing, snowshoeing, snowmobiling, and other outdoor enjoyment. Snow simplifies the landscape. A covering of snow provides a new look to familiar scenes.

And in late winter when the snow has melted and the streams are running free again, there are few fragrances as welcome as that moist freshness in the air that says, "spring!"

Each season in Minnesota has its own special sensation—something to anticipate: the return of songbirds and waterfowl in spring, the abundance of lush green growth and blue water in summer, the riot of color on trees and shrubs in autumn, the beauty of snowflakes and the graceful tracery of bare trees in winter. Without distinct seasons, the excitement of change wouldn't exist.

Les and I had happy childhoods, and our environment was part of the reason. I lived in Minneapolis near Lake Harriet where we kids hiked nearly every day in the summer to swim at the Forty-eighth Street beach. On Saturdays we often took a lunch and roamed along Minnehaha Creek or explored the marshes and pastureland around Diamond Lake. The Nicollet Avenue streetcar only went as far as Fifty-fourth Street then, and it was country beyond that.

Les, living in the small town of Moose Lake, was closer to wild country. He recalls that as a boy he would often get up early and hike along the Moose Horn River before breakfast and school, watching the ducks and other wildlife, learning to read tracks, and sharpening his powers of observation.

At the age of nine, Les placed a can with cross hairs on a ninety-eight-cent box camera and took his first picture of ducks in flight. Seeing an image of the ducks, however blurred they were on the drugstore print, determined his future career. He was going to be a wildlife photographer.

One summer during his high school years, he was a "savage" in Yellowstone National Park, working as a clerk and soda jerk. But on his "off" hours, he stalked big game with the family folding camera. Closer to home, he also gained outdoor experience through scouting and at YMCA Camp Miller at nearby Sturgeon Lake. Years of skiing through the woods and winter camping qualified him as an instructor in the ski troops in World War II. Ironically, his regiment was disbanded, and Les spent the last eighteen months of the war fighting in the jungles of the South Pacific with the Dixie Division.

Back home after the war, Les still aimed at being a wildlife photographer, but there were no organized college courses leading to a W.P. degree. So, on the GI Bill, he designed his own course which he thought would be helpful to his career and took it at night school: photography, writing, speech, art, some informal wildlife courses—and ceramics. That last course made the big difference in our lives. We met in that class and married after a brief courtship.

Portage Brook Falls, Arrowhead Trail. —L.B.

Les in the Voyageur. —L.B.

Canoe Trip Honeymoon, 1947

On October 25, 1947, Les and I set off on our honeymoon and my first canoe trip. I had assured everyone who doubted my sanity that if the weather was too bad we would change our plans, but inwardly I trusted my husband to take care of us no matter what.

My trousseau consisted of a pair of GI WAC shoes which cost four dollars at a surplus store, a pair of wool pants, a wool jacket, a wool ski bonnet, and a pair of leather "chopper" mittens.

I left my wedding orchid at Gunflint Lodge on the Gunflint Trail in midafternoon on October 27, and climbed into the canoe which we had ordered as a wedding gift to ourselves. Justine Kerfoot and Janet Hanson, who were partners in a canoe outfitting business there, had named our canoe the *Voyageur,* and on the bow seat had painted "To Fran from Les," and on the stern seat "To Les from Fran."

A few years later we painted the canoe red, and it was the bright spot of color among the blues and greens of Les's pictures which Hamm's Beer used in its advertising "From the Land of Sky Blue Waters." The red canoe almost became a Hamm's trademark.

We told Janet and Justine the route we intended to follow, and they said if we got snowed in they'd know where to send help. Little did we realize what

I find the constant flow of water reassuring. Shorelines rise and fall during wet and dry years, but I doubt that the flow of canoe country rivers has stopped completely since the glaciers melted. In times of drought, if we can hold out long enough, it will rain again. —L.B.

a wise precaution that was. Forty-four years later on October 31 and November 1, 1991, the worst snowstorm ever recorded in Minnesota dumped up to three feet of blinding snow, whipped by winds blowing thirty-five to fifty miles per hour. What turned out to be a blissful experience in 1947 could have ended in great difficulty, to say the least.

On our honeymoon voyage we followed the Canadian border route of lakes used by the French voyageurs from the early 1700s to the mid-1800s, in the remote country now known as the Boundary Waters Canoe Area Wilderness.

We paddled and portaged through Gunflint and Magnetic lakes, into the next small lake for our first campsite above Little Rock Falls. Huge, clean rocks sloped down to the water's edge. Tall pines towered above us. Clear, sweet, drinkable water swept past us to tumble over the rocks into the next lake. We were in paradise.

Les got a small fire going so we could cook our first meal on the trail. It was to be bacon and eggs. I thought he was taking a long time rummaging in the food pack before he confessed—he had left the meat package back in his mother's refrigerator. But we did have eggs. Cooking utensils had somehow been left behind, too, but Les quickly whittled some out of a piece of wood, and we still have them as souvenirs.

The mosquito season was long gone so we didn't need to put up a tent. As we lay that night looking up at the stars and full moon through the treetops, we thought of the French voyageurs who had camped in this very spot long ago, carrying copper kettles and trade items to the West, bringing back furs for the fashionable people in Europe. And we thought of the explorers before them who had traveled the old Indian routes in search of the Northwest Passage to the Pacific Ocean and Asia in quest of spices. These historic waterways remain almost unchanged by people in all the centuries they have traveled here.

The next day while Les was packing and loading the canoe, I lay down on a nice flat rock in the sun and promptly fell asleep. Les was considerate and fished below the falls and explored around camp until I was ready to move on.

That day was not only sunny and warm, but still. Not a breath of air stirred. I had never experienced such absolute silence before as we glided along. Our silence was rewarded when we came upon a dark brown mink loping over the shoreline rocks, completely oblivious to our presence.

The second day ended with a glorious golden sunset to our left as we paddled down Pine Lake (now called Clove) at the same time a yellow moon was rising over the trees on our right. And straight ahead was a wedding cake

Rainbows are usually associated with summer thunderstorms, but a waterfall mistbow happens every sunny day. Here is the unusual combination of fall color and the magic that happens when sunlight hits airborne drops of water. —L.B.

island for our camp.

The days were warm, but the nights were below freezing. Each morning our sleeping bags, as well as the trees, shrubs, and grasses, were frosted. That's why I had brought along my ski bonnet—for a nightcap.

After another unbelievably calm day in which we moved from lake to lake through clean waters and deliciously balmy air without seeing another person, the sun set before we found a campsite. As we entered Round Lake (now called Gneiss), we scanned the shoreline, and one rather light spot showed up. Les told me that you can always make camp on a sand beach, and so we headed for it across the lake. As the canoe slid up on shore, Les jumped out exclaiming, "Moose, bear, wolf, deer tracks! Wow! Look at them." I was looking, but my excitement wasn't filled with joy. If I could have walked home at that moment, I would have, and it might have been a short marriage.

Les promised to keep a fire going by our sleeping bags if that would make me feel better. I imagined I saw glittering eyes peering at us from the darkness, but no four-footed intruders entered camp, and sleep soon overtook fear.

During our honeymoon I found a new love—canoe country. I wasn't being fickle. I had just added a wonderful new experience to my life. Familiar as I was with most of Minnesota, I had never entered this wilderness of waterways before. It was completely unlike any other part of our state. We were truly on our own in a quiet, clean world of beauty.

Les and I returned to explore new canoe routes many times. Each time we were impressed by how precious, how fragile this wilderness is.

Before heading south to the town of Moose Lake where we were going to live, we roamed some of the back roads. The first night we spent in a deserted lumber camp off the Arrowhead Trail, inland from Hovland. It was owned by a friend, Vince Agurkis, who lived in Moose Lake. A huge pile of sawdust stood in the clearing. And since sawdust is good insulating material, Les had an idea. He dug into the pile a little ways and found it still had the warmth of August inside. So like two badgers, we burrowed into the sawdust until we had a cozy nest for ourselves and our sleeping bags.

And that wonderful aroma of warm sawdust! Few things stir the memory like fragrances, and the pungent smell of that pine sawdust transported me back to the age of eleven or twelve. My grandfather Eddy was a wholesale lumberman who took me with him one time to visit a lumber camp on the Saint Croix River east of Rush City. I was fascinated, watching the men walking on the logs jammed in the river, pushing and pulling with their pike poles, guiding logs onto the "bullchain" that carried them into the mill. Inside

With breathtaking views in several directions, the climb to the top of the Palisades on Seagull Lake is well worth the effort. And in season the blueberries on top are a dandy bonus! The grand, rugged scenery, the wildness, the cleanness, the rare, unspoiled virgin forest—all document the wisdom of preserving the Boundary Waters Canoe Area. This quiet wilderness can help a visitor get to know himself and his relationship to his world. —L.B.

the mill, the screeching and squealing of the saw that sliced off boards first from one side of a log, then the other, almost deafened us. But, oh, that wonderful aroma of fresh sawn lumber! Almost equal to the smell coming from the mess hall where I was allowed to eat a sumptuous meal of beans, meat, potatoes, vegetables, and pie with the men. No one ate heartier than the men in a lumber camp. This kind of camp belongs to an era that is all but passed, but the fragrant memory still lives.

Next morning in the deserted camp we were awakened by robin-sized gray birds calling to us. They were "camp robbers," "whiskey jacks," or, more properly named, gray jays, who frequent campsites where they can get a free meal. These were extremely tame birds and apparently very hungry, so much so that one hopped into the frying pan trying to steal a flapjack before we got it.

The next day of our northwoods honeymoon ended at the Cascade River on the North Shore of Lake Superior, now a state park. There was an undeveloped opening in the woods then and at that season we had it to ourselves for a camp. The river tumbles in a series of narrow waterfalls through a rock-walled gorge before it flows into Lake Superior just below the Minnesota Highway 61 bridge. Good trails follow the river, and a foot bridge crossing the canyon is used by deer as well as people. The lakeshore near the river is still one of our favorite places in a high wind when the waves are crashing on the jagged rocks. The rhythm of the ca-whumping and the after-splash are almost hypnotic, and I could spend hours happily mesmerized by the surf, watching gulls soaring and dipping overhead.

When the sun dropped behind the inland hills, we had to consider what we were going to use for our mattress that night. It turned out to be hay which we harvested from the abundant grasses in the clearing.

The finale to our honeymoon was a concession to our bond with civilization. We exchanged camp clothes for our wedding suits and drove to Duluth for lunch at a shoreline restaurant where we could watch huge freighters pass by.

Most of the shoreline of Lake Superior, the largest body of fresh water in the world, is still natural. Although there is almost constant movement of the water, varying from a light swish to the pounding of mountainous breakers, the basic shape of the pre-Cambrian rock shore has changed very, very slowly. —L.B.

The Metro: Minneapolis, Saint Paul, and Surroundings

Minnesota State Capitol. —L.B.

We start the exploration of Minnesota with the hub of the state—the area of the Twin Cities, Minneapolis and Saint Paul. The cities and their surroundings literally burst with things to do and see—theaters, concerts, sporting events, restaurants, museums and galleries, colleges and universities, the state Capitol complex, downtown business and retail centers, and shopping malls from small to "largest." You name it, there's something here for everyone. Newspapers and visitor guides feature dozens of current happenings, and the Minnesota Office of Tourism offers further help.

But one of the things that doesn't often get top billing is what makes the cities very special—their wealth of scenic green spaces. The winding Mississippi River threads its way through the very heart of the cities. One summer my brother worked on the tugboat *Demopolis* that pushed strings of barges between Saint Paul and Minneapolis. He commented on how, once he left the city centers, it was like boating through wild land, the river banks so steep and forested. Excursion boats now make the same delightful trip, and guides mention historic points along the way.

Parkways connect chains of lakes, golf courses, and beautiful spacious parks, and follow Minnehaha Creek to Minnehaha Falls made famous by the nineteenth-century poet Henry Wadsworth Longfellow. A trail at the base of

The Josiah Snelling *and its mate, the* Jonathan Padelford, *cruise the Mississippi through a flood-plain wilderness right in the heart of the Minneapolis–Saint Paul metro area. Deer, fox, raccoon, beaver, and many other species of wildlife frequent the winding shores within a few hundred yards of busy highways and business complexes.* —L.B.

Hiawatha and Minnehaha. —L.B.

the falls follows the creek through a glen to the Mississippi River.

Many buildings and places in the Twin Cities deserve special mention. The Capitol crowns one of Saint Paul's ten hills in stately fashion, at the end of a green, landscaped mall. Its huge marble dome, ornate carvings, and glass star on the floor of the rotunda, symbol of the North Star State, are some of the interesting features. But my favorites are the golden horses that prance heavenward from the rooftop.

The Minnesota Historical Society is a storehouse of the state's heritage. In 1992, a new and impressive home for the society was completed at the south edge of the Capitol complex mall on the south side of Interstate Highway 94.

Two homes owned and preserved by the state historical society in Saint Paul are the Alexander Ramsey House and the James J. Hill House. Alexander Ramsey, first governor of the territory of Minnesota, built his elegant home in 1872 at 265 Exchange Street. Most of the original furnishings decorate this fine example of the late Victorian period. The elaborate thirty-two–room mansion of railroad builder James J. Hill was built in 1891 at 240 Summit Avenue. Both homes are open for tours, but the Ramsey home may not be open in the winter.

The Science Museum of Minnesota is connected by skyway to the Arts

Henry Wadsworth Longfellow gave world renown to Minnehaha Falls in his poem, "The Song of Hiawatha." But this lovely cascade would have been well known without Hiawatha; after all, Longfellow knew of its beauty only from reading about it in his library in Massachusetts! Even though surrounded by the cities of Minneapolis and Saint Paul,

Minnehaha Falls performs in an idyllic setting, and the creek winds through a wild valley below the falls to its confluence with the Mississippi River. I photographed the scene with a 4 x 5 Speed Graphic camera using Ektachrome film, exposed for 1/25 second, to approximate the blur of the falls as it appears to the eye. —L.B.

Mendota Bridge. —L.B.

and Science Center at Tenth and Cedar streets in Saint Paul. Huge, prehistoric skeletons from the age of dinosaurs rub elbows with visitors who come to the exhibits, an incredibly realistic show in the Omnitheater, a special event, or classes. It's a busy place for the whole family.

The jewel of downtown Saint Paul is Rice Park, surrounded by the restored Federal Court House now named Landmark Center, the Saint Paul Public Library, and the elegant Ordway Music Theatre, home of the Saint Paul Chamber Orchestra, the Minnesota Opera, and the Schubert Club. Sweeping staircases in the Ordway lead to a lobby with giant windows overlooking the park and the Mississippi River. One winter evening after a concert, Les and I looked down on the park filled with glistening sculptures of ice made for the Winter Carnival and people viewing the figures. Lights in the park and other buildings made this a scene of other-world charm.

The Saint Paul Civic Center is transformed into a global village each year for the Festival of Nations. Ethnic entertainment, international cafés, handcraft demonstrations, and bazaars round out the activities. As part of the program one year, I led a children's chorus to celebrate Canada's Centennial.

Cafesjian's Carousel, a wonderfully restored, hand-carved masterpiece, is the center attraction in Town Square, Saint Paul's downtown indoor park.

My stomach urged me to stop waiting for just the right light and eat supper. But the late-setting summer sun was starting to cast purple tree-shadows across the sturdy face of the Sibley House, so I waited. The oldest permanent residence in Minnesota was built in 1835 by the man who was to become the state's first governor, Henry H. Sibley. Because of the late hour, I had this bit of history all to myself. It's easier to imagine the buck-skinned and top-hatted visitors of that period without modern cars and crowds of camera-flashers around. —L.B.

Lotus in bloom. —C.B.

I am particularly fond of abandoned pastures. The rich variety of plant life that carpets the land during the slow transition back to forest attracts the greatest possible diversity of animal life. From burly bears to tiny shrews, circling hawks to buzzing hummingbirds, voles and coyotes, foxes and grouse, snow buntings, redpolls, deer, moles, red-headed woodpeckers and bluebirds—all are drawn to, and thrive on, the old pasture. This classic grass-shrub-forest mixture is crowned by shining golden goblets—the American elm. —L.B.

Theodore Wirth Park. —N.B.

The Conservatory in Saint Paul's beautiful Como Park shelters magnificent plantings, some rare, that keep summer going all year-round. When the temperature outdoors falls below zero and the ground lies white with snow, a momentary trip into a lush, green world is a nice contrast. The zoo in the park is open all year free of charge.

The Minnesota State Fair, one of the largest in the nation, provides a super show of the best the state has produced during the year, from art to pigs, and quilts to apples. For ten days, ending with Labor Day, the crowds come to look, eat, show their products, see a horse show in the hippodrome, and attend the grandstand shows with big-name stars. I'll never forget paddling like mad at the end of a canoe trip one year so we could get to the fair in time to catch the Smothers Brothers show. We just made it.

The Gibbs Farm Home Museum at 2097 Larpenteur Avenue West, Saint Paul, traces the history of the Heman Gibbs family. Their first home was a log and sod shanty built on a claim along an Indian trail in 1849. Heman built this sturdy farmhouse over three decades, starting in 1854. The furnishings are typical of farm homes dating from about 1900. A barn containing early implements and an 1890 one-room schoolhouse are also on the property. Demonstrations are often given on Sunday afternoons of pioneer crafts such

Placed among the soft mounds of a northern hardwood forest, this small lake says "somewhere in central Minnesota." Non-Minnesotans might scoff in disbelief if you told them that the lake is in Minneapolis, but Minnesotans know that Minneapolis is the City of Lakes, so they wouldn't question it. Minneapolis it is, in Theodore Wirth Park. —L.B.

Immature Black-Crowned Night Heron. —C.B.

Snow-melt and spring rains provide a steady, slow flow of ankle-deep water through this black ash swamp. These are obviously ideal conditions for marsh marigolds, resulting in this grand display for about one week each spring. One feels there should be a festival to honor such a magnificent event! But there was no one else here as I picked my way in hip boots, trying to avoid crushing the showy blossoms. I tilted the lens forward on my 4 x 5 view camera to hold the entire field of flowers in sharp focus. —L.B.

Fort Snelling. —C.B.

as quilting, candle- and soapmaking, and sheepshearing.

Fort Snelling State Park is just a stone's throw from busy Minneapolis–Saint Paul International Airport, off Minnesota Highway 55. A visit to Historic Fort Snelling, first completed in 1825 and now reconstructed, provides a vivid trip back in time to how life was lived in the early days of the fort. It definitely wasn't fancy. Guides dressed as soldiers, or soldiers' wives, of the 1820s speak and act every bit as if they were living in the early fort. During a recent visit, the fort residents described life on this isolated, rugged frontier as we were seated on benches in the one-room schoolhouse. We climbed to the top of the famous round tower with its super-thick walls and well-placed gun holes. The baker was building a wood fire inside a brick oven and told us how many dozens of the hard, round loaves of bread he baked each day for the soldiers' rations. The blacksmith was hammering out a candle stand for the commandant's house. The woodworker was turning a chair leg with an ingenious homemade device, using a willow branch cut along the riverbank. The sutler sold us some spruce gum, a treat in those days.

For many years Fort Snelling was the only spot of Euro-American settlement in this vast area. Here, more than any other place, was the beginning of Minnesota as we know it.

While appreciating the cool shade of this silver maple in Fort Snelling State Park, I formed a frame with my hands and decided that there was a scene here worth photographing, of this quiet backwater of the Minnesota River. —L.B.

The entrance to the lower level of the state park is from Minnesota Highway 5 at the Post Road. There are places for swimming, boating, canoeing, fishing, hiking, snowmobiling, and skiing. The park includes Pike Island which can be seen from the Mendota Bridge at the confluence of the Mississippi and Minnesota rivers. Lieutenant Zebulon Pike (of Pike's Peak fame) met here with the Dakota (Sioux) in 1805 to purchase land for the fort for two hundred dollars worth of rum, some gifts, and a promise of two thousand dollars more.

A companion piece to Fort Snelling in Minnesota's early history is the Sibley House in Mendota just across the Mendota Bridge. A tour of this substantial stone house, built in 1835 by Henry Sibley, first governor of the state of Minnesota, can fill a fascinating afternoon. The Faribault House, built next door by Jean Faribault, an early fur trader, has a collection of rare Indian artifacts. Saint Peter's Church, up the hill, is the oldest church in the state.

The north side of the Minnesota River Valley, from Fort Snelling to Jordan, is the Minnesota River Valley National Wildlife Refuge. At the time of the authorization, Senator Hubert Humphrey said the area would "assure that the pressure of urban development will not deny future generations the opportunity to enjoy this irreplaceable natural asset." A wildlife interpretation and education center was dedicated September 1990 at 4101 East Eighty-eighth Street in Bloomington. A trail system follows the river, and there are opportunities for hiking, bird watching, photography, nature study, hunting, and fishing.

One of the "must" visits around the Twin Cities is to the Minnesota Zoo, termed a "major world zoological attraction." Creative planning makes it possible to see animals and birds in natural-looking habitats rather than in cages. You can watch dolphins cavort, beavers build dams, and approximately four hundred other species of the animal kingdom "do their thing" amid the lakes and rolling hills of the 480-acre park. Some of the more unusual inhabitants are Japanese snow monkeys, siberian tigers, musk oxen, Asiatic horses, bactrian camels, and moose. Animals can be petted and fed in the children's zoo. The zoo is south of the Minnesota River, east of Cedar Avenue on Johnny Cake Ridge Road in Apple Valley.

Also on the south side of the Minnesota River, just east of Shakopee at 2187 East Minnesota Highway 101, is Historic Murphy's Landing, a restoration project. The old Pond Grist Mill, fallen into disrepair, sparked the whole idea. The Shakopee Fire Department was going to burn it as a fire-fighting exercise, but before they got around to it, a local contractor who felt

Canada geese mate for life. The ganders are brave, dedicated, and effective protectors of their partners and goslings. I once made the mistake of wading between a goose and gander while filming the goose. All of a sudden I had a back full of biting, wing-beating gander that was not willing to accept my retreat without first delivering a memorable lesson. —C.B.

Early farm, Minnesota Valley Restoration Project. —L.B.

the building should be preserved put on a new roof and boarded up the windows, making it too valuable burn.

Margaret Mac Farlane, an art teacher in the Shakopee High School, became interested in the possibility of restoring the mill. She obtained a leave of absence to work on it, and the restoration grew from the mill that didn't get burned.

Murphy's Landing is a living museum of Dakota Indian dwellings, old log cabins, stores, a depot, and significant farms and homes that have been moved to this site and placed chronologically so visitors can walk from one decade to the next, from 1840 to the turn of the century. A large Indian village once existed here, and there are Indian mounds dating from 300 B.C. to the eighteenth century. From May to September, "residents" of the homes and "shopkeepers" demonstrate lifestyles of the period. A river nature trail adds another facet to this visit to the nineteenth century.

While you're in the same neighborhood, you may want to take in Valleyfair, with thrilling rides galore and entertainment, or you may want to try your luck at the parimutuel horse races at Canterbury Downs.

The Minnesota Renaissance Festival, four miles south of Shakopee on U.S. Route 169, is the scene of medieval ribaldry, food, fun, and fine crafts

Is there a more cheerful bouquet on the spring landscape than marsh marigold? Whether the day is bluebird weather or stormy, marigolds glow seemingly as bright. Large wetlands can contain acres of marsh marigolds, but even wholesale abundance can't detract from the specialness of these fresh beauties because they will all be gone, until next spring. —L.B.

weekends from mid-August to late September. You'll want to come early, prepared to stay all day.

In order to be a wildlife photographer, Les had to know the habits of the animals and birds: where to find them, their diets, their relationship to other wildlife, and their environment. It was a rather logical development that he became a consulting naturalist, too. He made studies of thirty areas in Minnesota that became nature centers, natural parks, or camps, giving his recommendations so that people could observe wildlife with as little interference with natural processes as possible. This means that wildlife must have protected places where it can live and have young, undisturbed by people. Humans can watch from blinds and paths, and as long as they do not intrude, wildlife will feel at home and remain.

Parks and centers open to the public in and near the Twin Cities that Les helped plan include: four Hennepin County park reserves, Hidden Falls Park and Crosby Lake Park along the Mississippi in Saint Paul, Bredeson Park in Edina, and Wood Lake Nature Center in Richfield.

Wood Lake Nature Center borders Interstate Highway 35W south of the Sixty-sixth Street exit. Right next to this busy highway visitors cross the cattail marsh on floating boardwalks, seeing ducks, geese, muskrats, herons, shorebirds, and other marsh residents at almost eye-to-eye range. Deer often have found their way through the city to Wood Lake. As Les says, "If the habitat is right, birds and animals will find it."

The Anderson Lakes area in Eden Prairie south of Interstate Highway 494, where we lived for twenty-three years, is being connected by wildlife corridors with the Hyland Lake Park Reserve in Bloomington and the Minnesota River Wildlife Refuge, providing summer and winter habitat for the large deer herd and other wildlife that live there. From our windows above Anderson Lake, we counted 174 different kinds of birds and many kinds of animals. One Easter morning was made very special by the sighting of a magnificent coyote.

Some of the most exciting moments happened when we had guests, and we were accused jokingly of staging them. Like the time we watched a hawk try three times before it caught a mouse on the ice in winter. Or when a seldom-seen shrike perched on a nearby birch tree. Or when a pileated woodpecker came to the suet two feet from the window for the first time, and the phone rang—*no one moved*. I'll never forget the first time I saw cormorants. They were

Early morning photography excursions are constant reminders of fall duck hunts with Dad when I was a boy. The thrill of getting up in the pitch black, before there was even a hint of dawn, of quickly downing a stack of Dad's special buckwheat cakes, of feeling our way to the car with the duckboat on the trailer and gunny sacks of decoys already in and ready, of speaking in hushed voices so we wouldn't disturb those still sleeping—all brought back.

This morning at the Carlos Avery Game Refuge would have been a good one for hunting—cool, cloudy, and with the promise of a good wind to keep the birds moving. And the memory of those mid-morning snacks of jelly-filled Bismarcks is still so fresh I can taste 'em. —L.B.

Burwell House, Minnetonka Mills. —L.B.

June, warm and moist, is the month of growth. Vegetation is at its greenest and fair weather clouds float by one beautiful day after another. Minneapolitans own this world of green and blue that encompasses their priceless chain of lakes. —L.B.

perched on dead tree stumps out in the lake, hanging their watersoaked wings out to dry after diving for fish. That was many years ago, and I thought it was a very rare sight until one spring when we saw hundreds of cormorants in western Minnesota.

In these large green spaces in and around the Twin Cities, people can relax, regenerate, and benefit, by just smelling the flowers and watching the sun set through the treetops, or by bicycling, ski touring, hiking, and participating in programs to learn more about the natural world we live in. Pretty terrific!

For those who love wildflowers—and who doesn't—the Eloise Butler Wildflower Garden in Theodore Wirth Park above Birch Pond in Minneapolis is the place to go. Most wild flowers native to Minnesota grow here in natural settings of wooded glens, marsh, and prairie—a bit of quiet space in the city.

Unlike many areas or buildings named for wealthy benefactors, the Eloise Butler Wildflower Garden was named for a retired botany teacher. After working without compensation to tend and preserve this wild wooded land, with other botany teachers, Miss Butler was made its first official curator in 1911 at a very modest salary. In 1929, the "Natural Botanical Garden" was renamed for her, and she continued to give the plants and birds loving care until her death in the garden in 1933 at the age of eighty-one.

One of our favorite visits any time of year has been to the Minnesota Landscape Arboretum, west of the Twin Cities on Minnesota Highway 5. The many varieties of trees, shrubs, and plants that grow in Minnesota are here in beautifully landscaped beds, or in wild prairie, woodland, and marshy pockets. A roadway winds through this extensive area, but to really appreciate what is there, the footpaths from parking areas are a better way to go. The impressive French chateau headquarters has an excellent nature library whose unusual tables are worth a visit by anyone who appreciates fine wood. The dining room is a delightful place to enjoy lunch by the fireplace or on the patio.

The Bell Museum of Natural History on the University of Minnesota campus, at University Avenue and Church Street, displays some highly prized animal and bird habitat exhibits with background paintings by Francis Lee Jaques, world-renowned wildlife artist. When Les was attending the university, he would take his bag lunch to the museum to chat with Jaques while he was working on a painting, blending the background imperceptibly with the specimens of fauna and flora in the foreground setting. Those hours led to a lifelong friendship with Lee and his wife, Florence. Before her death, she donated the Jaques Gallery to the museum along with several of her late

"Roses are red, violets are blue . . ." so the old rhyme goes, but the "Common Blue Violet" isn't blue at all, it's violet! And if I had my way, no beautiful wild thing would be called "common." That demeaning title should be reserved for the likes of house flies, not egrets, terns, and violets! There are about forty species of violets in variations of five or more colors, depending on how color-conscious you are. Most are violet, white, or yellow, but regardless of color, violets herald the welcome return of spring. —L.B.

husband's paintings. Minnesota is fortunate to have this legacy of a great artist's work.

The heart of downtown Minneapolis is the Nicollet Mall, a tree-lined lane accented with fountains, flower beds, and attractive lamplights. During the holidays the bare trees bloom with thousands of tiny lights, turning the mall, with its festively trimmed store windows, into a wonderland. Famous stores and specialty shops are centered here (many have branch stores in the suburbs), and a network of skyways makes it possible to go from one building to another, avoiding both traffic and weather.

I can remember when the Foshay Tower was built in 1929, modeled after the Washington Monument. Thirty-two stories in height, it was the tallest building in Minneapolis until the seventies when other monuments to business rose skyward, dwarfing the Foshay Tower, now a historic landmark. The graceful architecture of the Norwest Bank Building adds welcome variety to the tall buildings facing the mall.

At the lower end of Nicollet Avenue sits the Minneapolis Public Library with its innovative planetarium, and at the upper end, Orchestra Hall, built with superb acoustics for the Minnesota Orchestra, one of the world's fine symphonies. Nearby, Peavey Plaza hosts summer open-air festivities.

On the outer fringe of downtown Minneapolis, across Hennepin Avenue from Loring Park—that dollop of green and blue at the end of the mall—is Walker Art Center. It primarily shows avant-garde painting and sculpture in its antiseptic galleries. We have been delighted by some exhibits and completely turned off by others, but we're glad to have the chance to see them all.

Connected to the Walker is the Guthrie Theater. Its thrust stage was made for the famed Guthrie repertory company, but many concerts and other programs are also performed here.

Facing the Walker and the Guthrie is the Minneapolis Sculpture Garden, a serene green space for contemplation and enjoyment. Here everyone is free to roam, viewing creative pieces of contemporary sculpture in an outdoor setting. The giant "Spoonbridge and Cherry" fountain by Claes Oldenburg is world-famous. The Cowles Conservatory, on the west side of the garden, features a twenty-two-foot-tall "Standing Glass Fish" created by Frank Gehry, and shelters many botanical wonders from the elements.

The more traditional home of the arts is the Minneapolis Institute of Arts at Twenty-fourth Street and Third Avenue. It was remodeled in 1974 to house its own fine collections and visiting shows, and a highly creative Children's

Parks and nature centers strewn throughout the metro area protect a variety of ecosystems. This splendid display of late-blooming prairie flowers is in Bloomington's Richardson Nature Center. —C.B.

Heffelfinger Fountain, Lake Harriet Rose Garden. —L.B.

Theater. As adults we have enjoyed the plays as much as the children in the audience. Sharing the grounds is the Minneapolis College of Art and Design, which became independent from the institute in 1988.

Just down the street at 2303 Third Avenue, is the Hennepin County Historical Society Museum. George C. Christian, a Minneapolis milling executive, had this English Tudor mansion built in 1919.

Nearby, on Park Avenue and Twenty-sixth Street, is the American Swedish Institute. This castlelike mansion was built in 1907 by Swan Turnblad, the owner of the largest Swedish-language newspaper in the United States. It was probably built more as a showplace than as a residence, since the Turnblad family moved to an apartment across the street where they could live more simply. In 1929, the mansion was given to the Swedish Institute which Turnblad founded to foster Swedish culture in America. Allow time to admire the exquisite porcelain heating stoves, wood carvings, Swedish crystal, rugs, and the turrets, towers, and terraces.

Any time of year there are special events to attend in Minnesota. A complete list would be much too long to mention here, but may be obtained from the Minnesota Office of Tourism in Saint Paul. A few pulled out of the bag are Indian Powwows, often held on reservations, Buffalo Days in Luverne

I was there first, in the pre-dawn darkness, but it wasn't long before joggers and hikers appeared, and we all seemed to appreciate the beauty of this Lake Harriet dawn. —L.B.

with free buffalo burgers, horse and cutter parades in several cities, maple syruping at nature centers, Bean Hole Days in Pequot Lakes, and Agate Days in Moose Lake. But the biggest events, with the most hoopla, parades, contests, and queen candidates, are in the Twin Cities.

The Aquatennial in July in Minneapolis, the City of Lakes, features water-oriented sports and miscellaneous summer activities such as sand sculpturing and milk-carton boat races, in addition to two grand parades, balls, and crowning of a queen.

Saint Paul's Winter Carnival events go on no matter what the weather. Revelry abounds in the court of King Boreas, and speed skating, snowmobile and dogsled races, ice fishing, ice sculpturing, and skiing entice the hearty who only laugh at the wind and cold. Ice Palaces, turreted castles constructed of huge blocks of ice, have drawn the greatest attention in winter carnivals since 1886. In 1992, the tallest, most elaborate palace of all attracted millions of visitors and television viewers at the same time the football Super Bowl was in progress in Minneapolis. The Twin Cities had made it big, garnering worldwide attention.

The Metrodome in Minneapolis has been the site of many other major sporting events besides the 1992 Super Bowl. Twice, in 1987 and 1991, the World Series was played in the dome, and both times the Minnesota Twins won the championship. Minnesota boasts other professional teams, too—the Timberwolves basketball team, the North Stars hockey team, and the Vikings who made it to the Super Bowl four times.

The year 1992 saw the completion of another major attraction in the Metro area. The Mall of America, or "Mega-mall," is the largest enclosed shopping and entertainment complex in the United States. Imagine if you can, renowned retail stores, hundreds of specialty shops, a seven-acre amusement park, a walk-through aquarium, dozens of restaurants, nightclubs, fourteen movie theaters, and much more, under one giant roof. Located south of the airport, adjacent to Interstate Highway 494 and Cedar Avenue in Bloomington, this mall adds to the already established suburban malls and city-center retail stores, making the Twin Cities a mecca for shoppers and fun-seekers from this and other countries.

Trim in silhouette, exciting in such numbers, Lake of the Isles mallards have taken advantage of the refuge of the city lakes and the generosity of duck-loving city people who scatter corn and grain for the waterfowl. —L.B.

The Northeast

Minnesota's first bridge, Stillwater. —L.B.

Before leaving the Metro area of Twin Cities, drive northeast and get off the interstate highways to find the charming Saint Croix River towns. They possess a mellowed quaintness that makes them more precious as the years go by.

In 1848, the future state of Minnesota was born at Stillwater. Joseph R. Brown, one of Minnesota's most energetic pioneers, headed a delegation there to establish the Territory of Minnesota. Henry Sibley, the state's future first governor, was sent to Washington, D.C. to speak for them.

Lumbering was the territory's first great industry. Until 1914, logs floated down rivers to the Saint Croix boom site northeast of town. There they were sorted by the owner's mark stamped on the ends of the logs and rafted to sawmills. Today a never-to-be-forgotten experience is a fall canoe trip on the Saint Croix River, gliding downstream from Taylors Falls or William O'Brien State Park to Stillwater on a sparkling carpet of blue between walls of brilliant reds and golds. Canoe rental and pick-up service are available at all three points. Pocket parks, with sandy beaches on wooded islands, make ideal picnic spots.

Lowell Inn, a famous hotel and restaurant, dispenses hospitality and

One of the nicest things to happen between two states is the Saint Croix River. Very wild upstream, the Saint Croix is unspoiled, with few exceptions, all the way to its union with the Mississippi. And wonder of wonders, with few people and little industry along its banks and bluffs, the Saint Croix is perhaps the cleanest river of its size in the country excepting Alaska. —L.B.

Saint Croix River. —N.B.

fine food in a gracious setting. As thousands of other newlyweds have done, we spent our wedding night at Lowell Inn.

An intriguing self-guided tour of historic homes in Stillwater leads up the steep hills for glimpses of the exteriors of homes built in the heyday of lumbering. Some fascinating examples are "Grandma Bean's Playhouse," a parody on architectural styles; a house overlooking the river with a watchtower and siding resembling stone; one labeled "carpenter's frenzy;" and others with Italian, Moorish, Greek, Federal, and Victorian influence. The beautiful Washington County Historic Courthouse, one of Minnesota's oldest, stands on a lofty site at Pine and Third streets.

Another bit of the past has been brought to life in Stillwater by a train, the Minnesota Zephyr, which provides an elegant dining car experience while rolling through the scenic countryside. Riverboat rides are available too, or in your car follow what we consider one of the most beautiful drives in Minnesota, along the Saint Croix River.

This was the first Minnesota river to be preserved under the National Wild and Scenic Rivers Act of 1968, for having "outstandingly remarkable scenic, recreational, geologic, fish and wildlife, historic, cultural, or other similar values," for present and future generations. The Saint Croix

Situated in pastureland west of Stillwater, this maple took advantage of the available sunlight by growing out as well as up. —C.B.

Church in Marine-on-Saint Croix. —L.B.

lives up to all these requirements, and it was one of the original eight rivers in the nation to be approved under the act.

Few towns in Minnesota can match the quiet, undisturbed charm of Marine-on-Saint-Croix. An early sawmill town, it is desirable today as a lovely off-the-beaten-path place to live.

Taylors Falls offers a wealth of interesting old homes, too. The Folsom residence up the hill on Government Street, built in 1853, has been restored by the Minnesota Historical Society, and is open to the public on certain days.

State parks in Minnesota highlight the beauty of our state. Each of the sixty-five parks has been established for special reasons such as scenic beauty, history, geology, animal and bird life, and recreational opportunities. Guided or self-guided tours increase the enjoyment of what travelers see. Summer weekend programs appeal to all ages by featuring music, drama, demonstrations, storytelling, or live animals and birds. Major parks have daily programs. As much as Les and I think we know about our state, we are always delightfully entertained while learning more from these programs.

One of the most popular attractions in Minnesota for a day's outing

Despite the Saint Croix River's location adjacent to Taylors Falls, no expensive homes loom from the rocky outcrops, despoiling the view. For both the Minnesota and Wisconsin sides of the river here are state parks, keeping this spectacular area open to everyone. —C.B.

is the famous Dalles of the Saint Croix in Interstate State Park at Taylors Falls. This is a fantastic area of potholes created in prehistoric times when swirling waters of the Glacial Saint Croix River rotated boulders and pebbles in gigantic whirlpools, grinding away the volcanic rock. Glacier Kettle, one of eighty potholes, is sixty feet deep and twelve feet across. From launch rides on the Saint Croix River, some of the bizarre formations in the rock cliffs are visible, such as the eighty-foot-tall "Devil's Chair." Canoes can be rented, too, with pick-up service for a do-it-yourself river trip.

On the bank of the Snake River just west of Pine City is the reconstruction of a North West Company Fur Post. Documents and archaeological excavation revealed how and where the fortified post was built. A stockade surrounded one log building, measuring eighteen feet by seventy-seven feet and divided into several rooms. After only one winter's use, five hundred beaver skins plus muskrat, deer, and bear skins, wild rice, and maple sugar, obtained in trade from the Ojibway (Chippewa) Indians, were taken to the Fond du Lac collecting post on Lake Superior for eventual shipment to Europe.

The reconstructed post authentically duplicates the construction methods, crude furnishings, equipment, and simple life of the original post. We were offered some leftover beans still simmering on the open fire by one of the voyageur crew who spoke with an exaggerated French accent—maybe not an authentic French accent, but a colorful one.

Several rivers join the Saint Croix River in Saint Croix State Park, located east of Interstate Highway 35 on Minnesota Highway 48. This is one of Minnesota's larger parks with campgrounds, good fishing, and miles of hiking, biking, horseback, snowmobile, and ski trails. Visitors often see deer and other wildlife. One time Les came upon a young fawn crouched in the middle of a gravel road in the park. It remained still while he photographed it from all sides. He later modeled a clay figure of the fawn in the ceramics class we were both taking before our marriage. Les claims I fell in love with the fawn and that he came with it. Joking aside, the fawn (and Les) are still my prized "possessions."

One evening in Saint Croix State Park, our headlights shone on a whip-poor-will sitting in the middle of the road. Les suggested that I try to see how close I could get to it. I slowly walked in the shadows toward the bird until my hand almost touched it before I backed off. Its huge eyes and whiskers were almost frightening in appearance at close range, and

Whitetail fawns are about as lovable as an animal can be. But they all have mothers and should be left untouched! Not only is it illegal to take a fawn home, it is dangerous. Hand-raised deer grow quickly, and without fear of humans they are a problem. If loose, they are apt to be shot. And even though adult deer are beautiful and a delight to have around, the sharp-hoofed, sharp-antlered animals can, in an instant of frustration, do severe damage to people or other pets. —L.B.

Rural winter landscape. —L.B.

It's one of those magical mornings following an ice storm, when all the woods have been transformed into a shining filigree of crystal. Even the solid black trunks have been encapsulated in ice and are cold and smooth to the touch. The woods are clean, fresh, and filled with music—the tinkling, chiming notes made as the wind fractures the ice in the treetops. —C.B.

Swinging bridge at Jay Cooke State Park. —C.B.

anyway, I didn't want to alarm it.

West of Saint Croix State Park on Minnesota Highway 48 is the Grand Casino completed in 1992. It is one of several owned and controlled by the various Indian tribes in Minnesota. Further west is a giant indoor and outdoor flea market. At the junction of Highway 48 and Interstate 35 is a complex of tourist facilities—restaurants, filling stations, shops, and Mission Creek 1894 Theme Park where wood-fired, narrow-gauge steam trains transport visitors to lumberjack shows, a Dakota Indian village, a frontier town, and special events.

Banning State Park, just east of Interstate Highway 35 on Minnesota Highway 23, is a jewel in the rough. During high water levels on the Kettle River, kayakers test their skills with Hell's Gate, Dragon Tooth, and Ghost-town rapids, which descend between the rugged sandstone cliffs. Canoeists need to wait for low water levels. Old railroad beds left from the days when sandstone was quarried here and an old stagecoach trail make for easy and interesting hikes through the aspen and birch forest to lovely Wolf Creek Falls.

East of Carlton, Jay Cooke State Park is one of our most spectacular, especially when the Saint Louis River comes roaring through the jagged

Look. Look hard. The day after tomorrow these maple branches could be bare. Would I hold them if I could? No! It's the fleeting beauty that makes fall days so precious. Banning State Park. —L.B.

rocks. Standing on the swinging bridge that spans the river is one of the best ways to capture the drama of the scene. Minnesota Highway 210 leads to marvelous overlooks of the deep valley, and there are hiking trails from easy to difficult. The Willard Munger Trail, which begins in Hinckley on an abandoned railroad bed, links Carlton to Duluth for bicyclists and hikers.

Duluth is one of the most interesting cities in Minnesota, insanely built on the steep rocky hills rising above Lake Superior, the largest freshwater lake in the world. Sightseeing can be done on foot along the waterfront board walk where gulls soar; by horse-drawn carriage; by trolley, excursion train, or cruiser; by helicopter; or by car, especially along twenty-four-mile Skyline Parkway that winds six hundred feet above the lakeshore. Two stops on the drive are highlights: Hawk Ridge, one of the best spots in the nation for observing migrating hawks in the fall, and five-story Enger Tower where there's a great view from the top.

No visitor will want to miss the Marine Museum and Canal Park where it's almost possible to touch the huge ships loaded with iron ore and grain, many flying foreign flags, as they pass under the famous Aerial Lift Bridge and through the canal. The SS *William A. Irvin,* a former top-of-the-line ore boat now permanently docked, is open for tours. The chateau-like depot, now the county's Heritage and Arts Center, is a home for plays, ballets, concerts, and art exhibits, as well as housing a collection of antique trains, exhibits of early logging days, and memorabilia of a bygone era.

On the east end of the city, elegant Glensheen mansion is open for tours, and at the west end, the Lake Superior Zoological Gardens and Spirit Mountain for skiing and camping are special spots to enjoy.

Walleye, trout, and salmon can be caught casting from shore and piers, or if you choose, licensed guides on charter boats can help you land lunkers.

Two events that have brought national attention to Duluth are the Grandma's Marathon in June and the five-hundred-mile John Beargrease Sled Dog Marathon in January, named for a legendary mail carrier known for his dependable service in all weather.

Don't end your exploration of northern Minnesota at Duluth. Journey on. Only part of the beauty can be appreciated from a car. We like to park the car and hike the trails that follow the streams and rivers flowing toward the big lake. Gooseberry Falls State Park, one of the most

Split Rock Lighthouse, on Minnesota's North Shore of Lake Superior, is not the classic round, white spire often pictured on rocky coasts, but the old guardian is picturesque, high on its sheer cliff, preserved in a state park for its historic value as well as its handsomeness.

This photograph was made from a kayak. The spectacular cliffs and protected coves of the park's shoreline make this one of Minnesota's finest areas to explore from the water. —C.B.

Beaver River. —C.B.

popular parks, features a series of waterfalls plunging over layers of prehistoric lava flows. Split Rock Lighthouse, now preserved in a state park, stands in awesome splendor on a precipitous cliff above Lake Superior. Visiting the lighthouse and the other buildings gives one a glimpse into the early days of shipping on the Great Lakes. Trails lead to the Superior Hiking Trail.

The Superior Hiking Trail has been selected by the U.S. Forest Service as "one of the twelve best trails in the National Forests." When completed, it will be a 250-mile hiking path along the Sawtooth Mountain ridge, linking eight state parks and many resorts between Duluth and Canada. Rugged terrain with designated campsites and spectacular vistas are what hikers can expect. Volunteers maintain the trail, and the call is always out for more help.

If you haven't found any of the famed Lake Superior agates on the beaches so far, stop at some of the agate shops, such as those at Beaver Bay, to see or purchase a stone. Each one is unique.

A mountainous road leads to the top of Palisade Head for a breathtaking view from the sheer rock cliff high above Lake Superior. We have found blueberries growing among the rocks in early August. In fact,

There is something invigorating about standing at a high place and looking off to a horizon that disappears into infinity—something permanent about rocks and cliffs and about the motion of water. The combination of these things makes Palisade Head along the North Shore of Lake Superior a favorite place of mine. —N.B.

High Falls, Baptism River. —L.B.

blueberry patches occur over much of northeastern Minnesota.

Shovel Point, visible to the east from Palisade Head, has trails to the tip of the point where waves crash dramatically on windy days. From the point, there's a good view of the Sawtooth Mountain Range whose formation resembles the jagged teeth of a saw. Shovel Point and former Baptism State Park are now in Tettegouche State Park. Tettegouche encompasses several lakes and fourteen miles of hiking trails. The High Falls of the Baptism River, in the park and pictured on the cover of this book, can be reached by a hiking trail that joins the Superior Hiking Trail.

At Illgen City, travelers who don't like their roads always straight and wide will love Minnesota Highway 1 that dips and winds for sixty-three miles through forests and hills to the lake country of Ely and entry points into the Boundary Waters Canoe Area Wilderness (BWCAW).

Inland on Lake County Road 7, east of Finland, is George H. Crosby Manitou State Park, headquarters and takeoff point for backpacking trails and primitive campsites. This is a mountainous rock and forest park ending at Minnesota Highway 61 on the North Shore. Spectacular Manitou Falls on the lake side of the highway is on private land, but boaters can see it from the lake.

Built to be functional, but oh, how beautiful! Made from materials of the surrounding forest, log cabins and snowshoes were pioneer necessities. Today both still do their thing very well and give some of us a nostalgic closer tie to our Earth and our past. —L.B.

Temperance River. —C.B.

Many North Shore towns were first settled by Scandinavian fishermen who were drawn by the similarity to their homeland fjords. Their boats and fish sheds can be seen in some of the rocky harbors. Roadside stands often sell smoked and fresh fish.

Temperance River State Park has a narrow, steep gorge, cauldrons, potholes, and a series of waterfalls visible from the trail, well worth a stop and walk. It is the only North Shore stream without a "bar" at its mouth. Hence the name.

At Carlton Peak, the highest point along the shore, trails wind to the top for great views of Lake Superior and Sawtooth Range.

Beyond Ray Berglund Wayside, County Road 336 climbs away from the highway to a parking lot giving access to trails around Leveau and Oberg mountains. During the fall color season—September into October—the valleys and hills are a riot of color, making the hike a special experience.

Lutsen Resort was the first to be established on the North Shore. Lutsen and other area resorts now provide year-round recreation. Activities include golfing, downhill and cross-country skiing, horseback riding, alpine slide, gondola ride, and kayaking. The Superior Trail

Combine the spectacular autumn foliage of a mixed northern hardwoods with rugged rock outcrops of the Sawtooth Mountains and you get a combination that draws tourists by the thousands out of the cities and onto the hiking trails and country roads inland from Lake Superior. This view from Carlton Peak is just one of many that reward energetic hikers each fall. —C.B.

System links many of the resorts, from luxurious to rustic ones. To avoid disappointment, summer and fall-color reservations should be made well in advance.

One mile past County Road 41, look for a rather small fenced-in deer exclosure. Started in the 1950s, this demonstrates the difference in vegetation and growth within the fenced area where deer are excluded, from outside the fence where deer concentrate in great numbers in the winter to browse heavily on bushes and trees.

In Cascade State Park, the Cascade River drops nine hundred feet in a three-mile descent through a twisting, rock-walled gorge. Both deer and humans use a footbridge across the river.

Cascade State Park attracts large numbers of deer in winter. The climate near the shore is tempered by the lake and south exposure, and the snow is usually not as deep as it is inland, so this is where the deer "yard up" in the winter.

Les wanted to record how the deer at the Cascade yard fared during the winter to put it in a book to be called "Deer Diary." Harry Jones, a coworker of mine at the Minneapolis *Star Tribune* before my marriage, convinced Les to take a movie camera, too. So our savings went into the purchase of a sixteen-millimeter motion picture camera and food supplies. We made up many pounds of hamburger patties and froze them, and packed other foods that wouldn't be harmed by freezing.

We loaded the car with food and camping gear and drove up the North Shore of Lake Superior one shining winter day the first of February 1948. Lake Superior can be frozen one day and open the next depending upon the wind. Very seldom is it all frozen over. This day it sparkled blue, with white gulls soaring on the air currents and noisy old squaw ducks zipping above the waves.

In winter it's possible to see much further into the woods than in summer, when leaves on trees and bushes screen your vision. Beyond the city of Two Harbors, we began to see deer. Some were leaping away from the road with their tails waving like white flags. Others would watch us, ears alert, while some were undisturbed and pursued their business of finding tender tips of shrubs to nibble or standing on their hind legs to reach for branches. If a substantial part of a deer's diet is balsam, it means the deer may be close to starvation. Balsam fills their stomachs, but doesn't provide sufficient nutrition for deer.

It was evident by the number of deer we were seeing that many had

This fat fawn knows what's good for her! She's been nosing around in the soft snow for acorns. Thriving on her mother's milk, then being weaned to a large assortment of succulent plants and shrubs all summer and fall, and nipping twigs and digging for acorns during the winter, she has multiplied her weight at least ten times from her four to five pounds at birth. She isn't quite as fat as she looks, because her thin, red, white-spotted summer coat has been replaced with a two-inch blanket of hollow-haired insulation. Even so, she's a dandy nine-month-old deer, doing very well, thank you! —L.B.

moved to the shore from inland forests to yard up for the remainder of the winter. (On one trip we counted well over two hundred deer from the car, between Duluth and Grand Marais.)

At the Cascade River we parked and unloaded the supplies that were to keep Les fed, warm, and equipped to photograph deer for the next two months—snowshoes, a single burner gasoline stove, a mummy-type sleeping bag, mukluks and other boots, parkas and on and on. I drove back to Moose Lake, leaving Les to carry his gear to a protected opening far up in the woods.

On March 15, I returned by Greyhound bus. I was to film Les showing how he lived in camp and worked with the deer, to fit into the motion picture he was making. We thought it was a good time of year to do this; the sun was higher and days were growing longer and warmer.

Les hadn't set up our small GI mountain tent until my arrival. He had been sleeping under the stars on a bough bed on top of the deep snow. But as a concession to me, he put up the tent and built a fire for the first time. He believes that it's best not to depend on a fire for warmth; otherwise you won't want to leave it. So he dressed for the extreme cold and fared very well.

I had borrowed a parka and every piece of cold weather clothing I could lay my hands on, and I was ready for my visit to the woods.

Les's thermometer registered fifteen degrees above zero the afternoon I arrived—a nice balmy winter temperature. But the next morning, the mercury was barely visible at thirty-three degrees below zero!

Les learned in the ski troops that the best way to keep warm in a sleeping bag is without any clothing on. Socks and clothes are kept warm and dry by placing them between the inner and outer bags while you sleep. But there comes a time when one must bare one's body to the outer air in order to get dressed (or undressed), and the thin skin of our unheated tent didn't do much to keep out the cold.

Les got a fire going while I reluctantly forced myself to get out of the bag and dressed. At least in the deep woods the frigid northwest wind was slowed down considerably. Once out of the tent, clutching a steaming cup of coffee with mittened hands, I found myself edging closer and closer to the fire until I was almost in it, trying to absorb some of its warmth. I could see the fire and smoke, but I couldn't feel much heat. And somehow my usually cheery voice fell silent. As the sun rose higher but the temperature didn't, my spirits froze along with my feet. In spite of

Beyond the unbelievability of gazing at open water when the mercury has dropped well below zero is the sheer beauty of it. White curtains of mist rise and twist loose from the warm womb that bore them. The dance is a mesmerizing one. As I watch the ice, the water and fog playing their liquid round, all the lives and rivers and seals that this water has passed through seem to be flowing with it—the past bound to the future by a common drop of water. —C.B.

constantly pacing or walking, my feet were cold, and my boots, which were wrong for this kind of outing, froze with turned-up toes. I was miserable!

But thankfully, Cascade Lodge, on the North Shore about a half mile from camp, was able to accommodate us at night until the deep freeze ended three days later. My voice returned, and my spirits rose with the temperature. We snowshoed to the areas Les had worked with the deer, and I had fun being a cinematographer.

When the movie was completed, Les used it as a lecture film called, "I Lived with the Deer," for about two years. Later it was condensed to a ten-minute version with sound track, retitled "Deer Live with Danger" and distributed by Encyclopaedia Britannica Films.

Grand Marais is one of our favorite towns with an atmosphere different from any other. We like to browse the shops, eat at the restaurants, and enjoy the chance to be close to Lake Superior. Sailing instruction, charters for deep-sea fishing, and special trips to Michigan's Isle Royale are all available. The famous Gunflint Trail takes off up the hill to many lakes, resorts, outfitters, eastern BWCAW entry points, and winter lodge–to–lodge ski trails.

The Boundary Waters Canoe Area Wilderness is Minnesota's priceless treasure of hundreds of lakes bordering Canada where adventurers can paddle, portage between lakes, and camp. Because this is such a popular wilderness, restrictions and rules have been established, and between May 1 and September 30, permits for overnight stays (and motorized day use) are required. Outfitters have equipment to rent, information, and maps. Half the fun is planning and selecting the right food, clothing, and equipment, all necessary for a successful voyage into the wilderness.

Other trails that penetrate the wilderness are the Arrowhead Trail out from Hovland, the Caribou Trail from Lutsen, and the Sawbill Trail from Tofte.

One summer we worked on the lakes along these trails, making the Minnesota portion of a fishing film called, "Cast of Three." (The other two portions were filmed in Wyoming and North Carolina.) We sought photogenic sites and good fishing waters in all three states. In Minnesota's northeast or Arrowhead region, the possible locations were almost limitless and conditions close to sublime.

A popular hike in Judge C. R. Magney State Park leads to Devil's

What's around the next bend, the next, and the next . . . that's what canoe-tripping is. It's exploring country that has changed very little since the forest returned after the last great ice sheet melted. The world's finest canoe country, two hundred miles of shared wilderness between Minnesota and Ontario, is headwaters. Over the bulk of it there is only wilderness upstream, so the island-studded lakes and waterways are drinkable. That is a rare and beautiful situation, almost unique in the world. —L.B.

Devil's Kettle, Judge C. R. Magney State Park. —N.B.

Kettle where the Brule River divides. Half of it plunges in a fifty-foot waterfall; the other half disappears mysteriously into a pothole. Where that water goes has never been determined. The Brule is a good trout-fishing river as are many North Shore streams.

Grand Portage National Monument alone is worth a visit. As the name implies, this was the beginning of a long portage for the French voyageurs. They carried their trade goods or furs overland along the *grand portage* for nine miles to avoid the rapids and falls of the Pigeon River, which forms the border between Canada and the United States at this point. The trail, used by Indians long before the Europeans arrived, starts at a gap in the continuous hills on the lake shoreline.

Here on a protected bay of Lake Superior was the first European settlement in Minnesota. Inland exploration searching for a route to the Pacific, the sea of the west, had started here as long ago as 1679 when Daniel Greysolon, sieur du Luth, explored the region. The city of Duluth is named for him. Fort Saint Charles was established on Lake of the Woods in 1732 by Pierre Gaultier de Varennes de La Vérendrye, another early explorer. Many traders and explorers traveled the border canoe routes in the years after that, setting up innumerable trading posts. But it wasn't until

Within the Grand Portage Indian Reservation we not only come close to history, but we see what the land was like when history was made. For here we can find the largest stretches of undeveloped Lake Superior shoreline in Minnesota. —C.B.

1768 that the site of Grand Portage village was cleared and a fort built.

Every year canoes loaded with furs would arrive from inland wintering posts for the annual meeting at Grand Portage. Furs would be exchanged for supplies and trade goods which had been brought by large Montreal freighter canoes through the Great Lakes. Imagine also the exchange of stories—tragedies of lives lost in capsized canoes; illness (hernia was common); violence, whether from nature or humans; and rollicking tales of good humor. And songs, for voyageurs sang from morning to night on the trail and were often hired for their singing ability. And drinking, for this must have been a time for celebration and revelry. Once their business was transacted, the fur trading voyageurs returned to their inland wintering posts until the next year.

This was long before the days of government surveys and detailed maps of the labyrinth of waterways. But these men devised an interesting means of marking their routes through the lakes. A voyageur was chosen to climb a tall pine along the route. With an ax, he would chop or lob off the middle branches, leaving a great plume as a visible marker that could be seen from a long distance. Some of these voyageur lob pines have survived well into this century. A lob pine, cut by Boy Scouts on Crane

Lake, honors Sigurd F. Olson whose efforts were greatly responsible for the preservation of the border route wilderness.

The Grand Portage Fort has been rebuilt twice in recent times (the first restoration was hit by lightning and burned to the ground), faithfully following the original plans.

Les and I have paddled out into the harbor and tried to imagine how it would have seemed to approach the fort after the long, grueling, and often treacherous trip through the Great Lakes from Montreal. Even though the paddlers tried to hug shorelines, at times they had to cross wide stretches of open water where sudden storms could overtake them. The sight of Grand Portage at the end of their voyage must have been very welcome.

Inside the restored Great Hall, we saw an excellent film, depicting the rigorous life of the voyageur, and a tour of the buildings with a guide gave us a glimpse of how life was lived at the fort.

A trail leads up Mount Rose behind the fort for a panoramic view of Lake Superior. Twenty-two miles from shore, Isle Royale sometimes appears to float on the distant horizon. You can also hike all or part of the Grand Portage trail as we have, and try to imagine carrying two ninety-

As I look down on the Great Hall of Grand Portage National Monument from up here on Mount Rose, after a warming climb on snowshoes, I wonder how different the scene would have been when this was a fur trade center. The old fur post here on the North Shore of Lake Superior is being reconstructed as it was in the Eighteenth and early Nineteenth centuries. Sixteen more buildings within the stockade will match as closely as possible the original busy center.

Grand Portage was the meeting place of large freight canoes from the east and the tough little voyageurs who paddled and portaged furs here from a tremendous area north and west. The nine-mile Grand Portage Trail, bypassing waterfalls on the Pigeon River, tied Grand Portage to literally thousand of miles of wilderness canoe trails. —L.B.

The Witch Tree. —C.B.

pound packs on your back. That was standard (some carried more) for the sturdy little Frenchmen who were among the first white men to venture this far west.

On Hat Point in the Grand Portage Reservation, an ancient, gnarled cedar tree grows inexplicably from the shoreline rocks. Now known as the Witch Tree, it has held spiritual significance for centuries for the Ojibway who live on this land, and for modern observers it is an awesome example of perseverance, creating a profound sense of respect and inspiration.

Grand Portage State Park, one of our newest state parks, allows visitors to view the spectacular High Falls of the Pigeon River from the Minnesota side. (Previously the only public viewing was from a rather precarious point on the Canadian side.) Trails lead to great overlooks, but there is no camping.

The International Bridge on Minnesota Highway 61 is one of the few road entry points into Canada from Minnesota. There isn't another bridge until International Falls two hundred miles to the west, or the Sault Locks to the east at the end of Lake Superior. This is big country with lots of trees, water, and wildlife creating a wonderful wilderness.

Shared with Ontario, the High Falls of the Pigeon River is Minnesota's highest waterfall. It is one of several falls that created the need for the Grand Portage that connected Lake Superior with the inland canoe country. —C.B.

To get to Ely and the west end of the BWCAW from Grand Portage State Park, either get in a canoe and paddle like the voyageurs did, or backtrack down Minnesota Highway 61 to Minnesota Highway 1, and then northwest to Ely.

Ely retains the atmosphere of a frontier town Minnesota-style. Outdoorsmen and -women, wearing boots and flannels rather than urban duds; canoes and outfitters; lumberjacks; sled dog mushers; snowmobilers; and informal hospitality are apparent everywhere. This is the heart of takeoff points into the BWCAW, so it isn't difficult to find information, maps, guides, and gear for a wilderness adventure.

Many snowmobile trails are in the area, the longest being the Taconite Trail from Ely to Grand Rapids, 170 miles, and the Arrowhead State Trail from Tower to International Falls.

Outside the towns are thrilling sights that can often be the highlight of a vacation. They aren't scheduled, and there's no guarantee you'll see them—that's what makes the sight of any animal in the wild a special event. Even though Les and I have spent many years camping and observing wildlife, the excitement of watching *any* animal or bird, large or small, has never worn off. But I've discovered the bigger the animal, the harder my heart pounds.

The monarch of our wilderness is the moose, who likes to feed on tender branches and leaves of trees and bushes and on swamp vegetation above and under the water. We were surprised once to see a calm pond explode when a moose surfaced from feeding on pond lily roots. It's hard to comprehend how large a moose is until you get too close for comfort. They stand six to seven feet at the shoulder and weigh up to fifteen hundred pounds. The male has a "bell" hanging from his neck and grows a pair of broad antlers each year. These are covered with a velvety skin until fall when he polishes them, ready to fight for a female. We might consider the cow moose ungainly, with her hump back and huge nose, but a bull is willing to risk his life in battle for her. During most of the year, moose will avoid human confrontation but in autumn the male may charge unexpectedly at anything that disturbs him—even railroad locomotives.

The graceful white-tailed deer is Minnesota's other antlered animal, red and sleek in its summer coat, gray in its winter coat of hollow insulating hairs. We think this is the most beautiful North American animal, and our spines still tingle when we spot one, or a group, nibbling in a field near the edge of a woods as we slowly drive down a country road just before

Free again of its winter casing of ice and snow, a northern stream sings a happy song of spring. A late snowstorm could again drape the forest in a foot-deep blanket, but the stream will remain open and any set-back will be brief. —L.B.

sunset. Chances of seeing wildlife are usually best from a car, as many animals are accustomed to them. The sight or scent of a moving person can send them leaping or scurrying for cover.

When I'm apprehensive about meeting up with a bear in the woods, Les keeps telling me I'd be lucky to ever see a bear. That statement usually would be true in the winter when bears are hibernating, but I don't know how "lucky" campers feel when a prowling black bear makes off with their food supply. I'll have to admit it's true, though, that, other than the bears who have learned that certain campsites are free cafeterias, they will avoid contact with humans and usually run away.

Another denizen of the deep woods that is rarely ever seen but is sometimes heard "singing" is the gray or timber wolf. It is the much maligned and misunderstood "villain" we hear about in childhood fairy tales, and the image is hard to change. Recent studies have shown what a remarkable, intelligent animal the wolf is, living in a very structured, well-regulated society. Northeastern Minnesota is the only area in the lower forty-eight states where wolves still thrive. The International Wolf Center in Ely has exhibits, maps showing the location of packs, live wolves, and other fascinating opportunities to become better acquainted with timber wolves.

For many people vacationing in northern Minnesota, the most thrilling and memorable sight is a display of aurora borealis or northern lights. There is no describing the wonder of these shifting colorful patterns of light that leap and dance in the night sky in absolute silence.

Southwest from Ely are the great iron ranges of Minnesota—the Vermilion, Mesabi, and Cuyuna. At Tower-Soudan, the deep underground mine was closed in 1962 when the rich ore deposits ran out. The mine and over a thousand acres were donated for the Soudan Underground Mine State Park. The elevator ride down 2,400 feet, followed by a three-mile train ride through a mining tunnel, is a unique experience in Minnesota. We were fascinated just watching the man skillfully manipulating the complex controls that run the elevator. He and many of the guides were former miners.

The largest mines are open pit mines, because iron-bearing strata occurs near the surface. Looking over these vast pits is something akin to a view of the Grand Canyon. The world's largest open-pit iron mine can be seen from the Hull-Rust Viewpoint located near Hibbing. The view over the Rouchleau Mine at Virginia, called Mineview in the Sky, is from

He's called a brush wolf in the north woods, but he's really a coyote, and he ranges far beyond his traditional prairie home. Welcomed by cattle raisers for controlling rodents, hated by sheep ranchers, the controversial little wolf has gotten lots of folks mad at each other. Persistent poison 1080 (now banned), aimed at the coyote, killed thousands of non-target animals and birds such as the golden eagle. And that really got folks upset! In spite of intensive trapping and poisoning, the coyote has thrived and now roams over most of North America. —L.B.

a twenty-story stockpile. The gigantic equipment used to dig and haul ore looks like toys from a distance, but at close range they are monsters. Information centers are located at many points throughout Range cities to guide visitors.

Bus tours to points of interest are available at Hibbing. The Paulucci Space Theatre with wrap-around movies, and singer Bob Dylan's home are both here. The Hibbing High School was built with many elegant features purchased with money from the mining industry.

Ironworld U.S.A., between Hibbing and Chisholm on Minnesota Highway 169, is on the brink of the old Pillsbury mine. Creative displays give the visitor a grasp of iron mining and taconite production, and the hardy folks who mined the ore. Music, dancing, special events, ethnic foods, and crafts can fill a day with fun and learning. In Chisholm, the Minnesota Museum of Mining is well worth a visit, too, with a simulated trip through a mine, an "old town," and the chance to climb up on some monstrous mining equipment.

In Eveleth, hockey fans will want to visit the U.S. Hockey Hall of Fame. And skiers will find groomed cross-country trails and fifteen downhill courses at Giants Ridge near Biwabik. There are also many other first-rate ski areas scattered through the state. The fifty-two-mile Laurentian Snowmobile Trail from Biwabik connects with others to give plenty of variety to winter adventures.

From a high point southwest of Chisolm, the water flows in three directions: north to Hudson Bay, east to Lake Superior, and west to the Mississippi River.

Hill Annex Mine State Park off U.S. Route 161 in Calumet is on the National Register of Historic Places. The large open pit produced sixty-three million tons of ore during its sixty-six years of operation which ended in 1978. Now summer visitors can take a tour bus down three hundred feet into the mine pit which has a 250-foot-deep lake at the center. Guides (many former miners) explain the equipment and techniques used to bring out the ore and send it on its way to ore boats on Lake Superior and eastern steel mills.

Grand Rapids is famous for its forest products industries and for being the birthplace of Judy Garland. A collection of Judy memorabilia is in the County Historical Museum. Tours of the Blandin Paper and Wood Products Companies focus on today's forests and paper-making technologies.

An authentic 1900 logging camp has been recreated at the Forest History Center just southwest of Grand Rapids. The camp blacksmith, lumberjacks, and other workers in the camp tell how they lived and worked, and visitors can try some of the hands-on activities. An added attraction is the moored

There are many flowers that are more colorful and showy than blueberry blossom, but few promise taste treats to equal wild blueberry pie! —L.B.

Evening grosbeak. —L.B.

wanigan on the river—a cook shack and store that accompanied spring log drives down to saw mills. Trails through a forest of birch, maple, and pine allow colorful views of the Mississippi River.

Another delightful facet of a visit to Grand Rapids is the Showboat on the banks of the Mississippi. Variety shows of the 1800s are performed the last three weekends of July at nine o'clock at night.

On the Minnesota-Ontario border east of International Falls is Voyageurs National Park, named for the French-Canadians who transported furs and supplies along this water highway. (We first "met" them at Grand Portage National Monument on Lake Superior where their trips by canoe and portages into the interior started.) Thirty beautiful lakes, large and small, fill rocky glacial basins. One of the best ways to experience the vastness of the park and see its wildlife and scenery is aboard a boat tour led by naturalists. Or you may choose to ride in a voyageur canoe replica with costumed interpreters telling tales and singing songs of the fur trade days. There is excellent fishing in the park, and eagles, loons, beavers, deer, and other wildlife are not uncommon sightings.

International Falls is a bustling wood-products center with plant tours available. It has become known as the "Ice Box City" because winter temperatures are often the coldest in the nation. One of the few bridges linking

If ancient pines in Voyageurs National Park could speak, they would have colorful tales to tell. They were here when the voyageurs came paddling by, singing their French cadence songs. —L.B.

Canada to Minnesota crosses the Rainy River here.

Shortly after the turn of the century, my father signed up for a homestead on the west fork of the Black River and took the train to International Falls from Minneapolis. From the Falls he traveled down the Rainy River by steamer to Loman, a single house that served as post office. From Loman he had to walk nine miles to his claim at the end of the trail. He was a young, city-bred minister's son with no knowledge of the north woods or cabin building.

As a child I never tired of hearing about how his neighbors on the trail helped him build his cabin and barn before winter set in and how his winter's supply of potatoes and vegetables froze when his woodstove went out, as well as other experiences of northwoods survival.

The first night he spent in the cabin he thought he heard shooting outside, only to learn later that it was beavers slapping their tails in the water. Isolation was new to him, and he soon grew so lonesome he sent for the family dog. But the dog was lonesome, too, and his endless howling only made matters worse. Dad finally shipped him back to Minneapolis.

After six months the claim was legally his. He "proved up," went back to Minneapolis, married my mother, and settled down to an urban life, his taste for adventure apparently satisfied.

When I was in high school, our family took a camping trip through northern Minnesota. We went to Loman, and the same couple were running the post office in their home. They remembered Dad. We wanted to hike in and see if his cabin was still there. They told us all the claims had been deserted and the trail grown over so we couldn't get through. Although I have seen many tumbling-down homestead cabins in northern Minnesota, relics of shattered dreams and hard work, I still have a hankering to see Dad's place.

Seventeen miles west of International Falls, at the junction of the Big Fork and Rainy rivers on Minnesota Highway 11, is Grand Mound interpretive center. The oldest of five burial mounds dates back to archaic Indians who probably began camping here about 5,000 B.C., fishing for enormous sturgeon. Later groups used the area as evidenced by their tools and other artifacts in the distinctly dated layers of earth deposited by flooding. Grand Mound, the largest mound made of ninety thousand cubic feet of earth, is the Upper Midwest's largest prehistoric structure, and one of Minnesota's most significant archaeological sites. There are nature trails, picnic tables, and audio-visual programs to tell the story of past cultures and their environment.

As I was walking a woodland path near our home, a movement near the ground caught my eye. I knelt down to see what was moving the vegetation, and discovered that some of the leaf movement was not leaves at all, but this just-emerged luna moth. From its cocoon on the ground, the moth was climbing a stem with enough clearance to spread its great wings for the first time.

Thinking it would rest there, I memorized the spot and dashed to the house for a view camera and tripod. Still there. I kept an eye on the moth while I uncased and set up, then composed the picture under a black cloth. The lens was just inches from the lovely moth, but the shock of emergence was still its primary concern, so it posed quietly while I took its picture. —L.B.

The Northcentral/West

My first year after graduating from the University of Minnesota in 1936, I taught in Baudette on the Rainy River. Driving through mile after mile of the Big Bog (that large blank space on a geographer's map) to get there, I felt I was going to the end of the world. I have learned since to appreciate the fragility of bogs and their importance in our ecosystem, and so I could look at it quite differently today. The lake where we now live has a floating bog shoreline where vegetation such as alder, sedges, and even tamarack trees form mats not rooted in soil. Several sizable islands of vegetation have broken off from shore, so during summer our scenery changes every day depending on wind direction.

From Baudette, where I had a great year learning to know a very wild part of our state and a lot of fine folks, there is easy access to Lake of the Woods, a favorite of anglers, from either the U.S. or Canadian sides of the border.

Once there was no road to that isolated piece of Minnesota called the Northwest Angle that sticks up like a thumb at the top of the state map. Through a quirk in establishing the U.S.–Canadian boundary back in 1783, this small piece of Minnesota is surrounded by Canada and Lake of Woods. Most of the few people living on the angle liked their isolation, when access was mostly by boat or seaplane, but now, like it or not, there is a road approach from Warroad.

Fort Saint Charles, the fort and fur trading post of French explorer La Vérendrye in the early 1700s, has been restored. It is on Magnuson's Island just off the angle shoreline.

Traveling westward, the land flattens out. This is the Red River Valley, part of the lakebed of prehistoric Glacial Lake Agassiz which at one time was one to six hundred feet deep and larger than all of the Great Lakes combined. Upper and Lower Red lakes and Lake of the Woods are remnants of this ancient lake. The Glacial River Warren flowed south from the lake, cutting through the continental divide at Lake Traverse and carving out the broad Minnesota River Valley.

The black topsoil in the old lakebed is deep and some of the most fertile in the world. Farms are large here. Fields of sugar beets, potatoes, wheat, barley, oats, sunflowers, soybeans, and onions stretch to the horizon across the level landscape. My first reaction at seeing such flat land was almost the same as when I first saw mountains. They are both vast and awesome. Mountains can almost overpower with their height; here the land seems endless, topped with a huge, open sky. Only farm buildings,

As the last glint of gold leaves the snow, and the silhouetted spruce blend into the dark of night, I must leave this northwoods bog. My fingers have grown numb fumbling with the frozen metal of my camera, and my eyes cannot penetrate the darkness. I am out of my natural environment and in that of the bog creatures. Soon in this winter fairyland, tales will be written in the snow—of ruffed grouse diving into insulating fluff to spend the night, ready to explode from their shelter if danger threatens; snowshoe hares hopping about beneath the protective spruce, pursued by coyotes or possibly timber wolves; mice scurrying about in their tunnels, and a red fox trotting nose down in search of them, hoping that each leap into the air will land on dinner, taking several tries to secure at least a one-mouse supper—a whole series of life and death adventures, clearly told by the tracks to be read the following morning. —C.B.

visible from miles away, emerge from the landscape.

We were just lucky to be at Old Mill State Park northeast of Warren on Labor Day when the steam-powered mill is fired up to grind grain for neighboring farmers. They stood patiently in line with their bags of grain, because "you can't get better flour anywhere else." The friendly camaraderie made it seem like one big family reunion. We experienced that same friendly spirit everywhere, though. Maybe that's the mark of a Minnesotan—friendly.

At the Old Crossing Treaty Site, west of Red Lake Falls, bands of Ojibway (Chippewa) Indians ceded almost ten million acres of fertile land in northwestern Minnesota and northeastern North Dakota to the U.S. government in 1863. The treaty site was on the Red River Oxcart Trail, one of the state's first important roads. Caravans of creaking two-wheeled carts drawn by oxen transported furs and other goods from Red River settlements to Saint Paul, and carried supplies from the city on the return trip. A huge cottonwood tree in the park was used as a "post office," where messages were left to be picked up or were delivered by those passing by.

In 1931, a repair crew working U.S. Route 59 north of Pelican Rapids uncovered the skeleton of a girl about fifteen years of age. Dating the skeleton has proven difficult work, and estimates range widely. If it were as old as the glacial deposit it was buried in, about ten thousand years, then the skeleton would be the oldest known in North America. The skeleton, initially dubbed Minnesota Man and later renamed Minnesota Woman, with a marine-shell pendant and elk-antler tool found with her, are owned by the University of Minnesota. A highway marker stands at the site of discovery on the lakebed of ancient Glacial Lake Pelican.

Buffalo River State Park, east of Glyndon, is on the wooded Buffalo River as well as prairie land. This prairie, where 250 species of wildflowers and grasses grow, is adjacent to the Nature Conservancy Bluestem Prairie Scientific and Natural Area, together forming the largest and best of the state's prairie preserves. Campbell Beach Ridge, a remnant of ancient Lake Agassiz which once covered this area, runs through the park. There is a great diversity of animal, bird, and plant life, from white-tailed jack rabbits and prairie chickens to purple coneflowers.

In Moorhead, the Heritage Hjemkomst Interpretive Center houses a replica of a Viking ship built in Hawley and sailed across the Atlantic to Norway. The Comstock House, built in 1882, was the home of two noted Minnesotans: Solomon Comstock, political figure and entrepreneur, and his daughter Ada Comstock, who was the first dean of women at the University

Anyone who has walked out onto the prairie in the still-dark morning, then waited quietly for hours in a blind, knows the rush of excitement brought on by the first "booming" of the prairie chickens. Each spring the males congregate at a booming ground, courting females by displaying and calling. It is a dramatic part of spring in Minnesota that is no longer heard in most of the prairie chicken's original range. —C.B.

Frosted Norway pine and oak. —L.B.

Exploring is part of the joy of photography. I found a treasure of perfect showy lady's slippers in Chippewa National Forest. —N.B.

of Minnesota, and later, president of Radcliffe College from 1923 to 1943. Guided tours tell about the Comstocks and the Red River Valley.

Stick a pin almost anywhere in the map of northern Minnesota, and you'll probably hit a forest, a lake with good fishing spots and swimming beaches, a golf course, a resort, a summer cabin or campground, or a town or city that caters to vacationers. This is the promised land for thousands of folks who are drawn northward by sparkling lakes and rivers and opportunities to relax and enjoy the great outdoors.

This is the land of the legendary logger, Paul Bunyan, where forests of giant pines were cut and floated down rivers to lumber mills. The days of the big log drives are over, but the memory of Paul is kept alive in Brainerd and Bemidji where huge statues of him are almost "life size." We have seen his "girlfriend" at Hackensack and his "birthplace" at Akely. All the lakes are allegedly hoof prints of Babe, his Blue Ox. Thanks to Babe, but more likely the glaciers that once covered Minnesota, there are some whoppers, like Mille Lacs, Leech, Cass, Upper and Lower Red, Winnibigoshish, Rainy, and Lake of the Woods. In between lie literally thousands more of lesser size but no less beautiful.

A taste of what a "real" logging camp was like can be sampled at the Rapid River Logging Camp north of Park Rapids where meals are served in the cook shanty lumberjack-style.

Itasca is the queen mother of Minnesota's state parks, established in 1891 to preserve the true head (*verITAS CAput*) of the Mississippi as determined in 1832 by the expedition of Henry Schoolcraft who was guided by an Indian.

Even though many visitors come to Itasca State Park for the experience of "stepping across the Mississippi River" on the boulders where the river leaves Lake Itasca to begin its 2,552-mile journey to the Gulf of Mexico, a visit to the park should include some of the other features that leave wonderful lasting memories.

These are: walking trails under towering pines, many over two hundred years old; the tallest red (Norway) pine, over 120 feet tall and over three hundred years old, on the Big Pine Trail; nearby, the tallest white pine in the state; the bison kill site where excavations of bones of an extinct bison much larger than today's buffalo and artifacts indicate that nomadic hunters ambushed bison as they forded the stream seven to eight thousand years ago; historic log buildings and Indian mounds; campfire and other naturalist programs; swimming, camping, and more.

People come, as if on a pilgrimage, to step across the small stream flowing around boulders from Lake Itasca. They take pictures of each other balancing precariously on the slippery rocks to put in the family album as a reminder of this historic moment. For this is the source of the Mississippi River which flows from this point over 2,300 miles to the Gulf of Mexico.

An estimated million visitors come to Itasca State Park each year, not only to walk across the Mississippi, but to enjoy the magnificent forest of towering red and white pines, to hike the trails, observe and learn about wildlife, fish, camp, picnic, dine at Douglas Lodge, or just "get away" from the routine of life back home. —L.B.

The Park Rapids–Detroit Lakes area leaves little doubt why Minnesota is called "land of lakes." Minnesota's supply of water is unequalled by any other state (one square mile of water for every twenty of land). Resorts large and small cater to vacationers on the dozens of lakes concentrated in this section of the state.

Smoky Hills Artisan Community fulfills the dream of a group of women to create a market for their talents. They were able to get financial backing, and the result is a charming colony of individual cabin-shops nestled in a woodland setting and connected by a covered boardwalk. From Memorial Day weekend through Labor Day, visitors can stroll from shop to shop watching artists work at their crafts, or try hand-dipping candles or tie-dyeing T-shirts themselves. A wide variety of crafts, including Indian beadwork and jewelry, outdoor demonstrations, dressing up for Old-Tyme Photos, and a meal at the restaurant, fill a day before you know it. We bought a decorative piece woven from Norway pine needles after watching a woman make it while her husband prepared more of the long needles from Minnesota's state tree. The community is located on Minnesota Highway 34 near Osage, nine miles west of Park Rapids.

A two-hundred-pound stone tablet found in 1898 near Kensington tells in runic carving of an exploration journey in 1362 by eight Swedes and twenty-two Norwegians. Some scholars have called it a fake, while others have defended its authenticity. The stone itself may or may not be a true record of an early expedition, but there is other evidence we have seen that leads me to believe that at some time Norsemen explored this land. Mooring stones, such as the one in the park at Hawley, have been found along a waterway from Lake Winnipeg in Canada to Sauk Centre. They are similar to ones found in Massachusetts and Delaware and along lakes and fjords in Norway and Sweden. In each large stone a triangular-shaped hole slants downward toward the lake so that a ring bolt or pin could be held securely for mooring a sizable boat. When we were in Hawley we learned that one of these stones was found at the site of the Kensington runestone and that a stone at Cormorant Lake was looked for and found because of the message on the runestone. A Viking sword, firesteels, axes, and spearheads have been unearthed, all adding to the intriguing mystery. Wouldn't it be great if someday the hull of a Viking ship was found on a lake bottom! That would be the key piece to the puzzle. Meanwhile, Alexandria, proclaiming itself the "birthplace of America," guards the runestone and other artifacts in its museum, and

Itasca State Park has miles of roadside beauty, but I'm always curious to know where hiking trails lead. This morning the trail led to a quiet glen with some of the large pines for which Itasca is known. In this very popular and populated park I had the glen to myself. —N.B.

Minnesota farm. —L.B.

displays a giant replica of it in a highway park. A statue of the "world's tallest Viking" stands in the heart of town.

Some special events in this part of Minnesota include rodeos and horse shows, steam threshing bees, fishing contests, golf tournaments, and summer theater. Potholes and fields make for excellent duck and pheasant hunting. Two scenic lookout points are Inspiration Peak, a state wayside park west of Parkers Prairie, and Mount Tom in Sibley State Park north of Willmar. Indians once burned signal fires on Mount Tom, which is the highest point in fifty miles. We remember the town of New London, nearby, as one of the most charming in the state. The federal fish hatchery there stocks lakes of the region.

The section of Minnesota lying west and northwest of the Twin Cities is as well-known for prosperous farms as for vacation lakes. This is not the north woods; forests are apt to be oak, basswood, and maple rather than pine, spruce, and balsam. But the lakes are just as great for fishing, swimming, and boating; most are rimmed with year-round or summer homes and resorts. One year we filmed a fishing movie called "A Bass in the Hand," and got well acquainted with the lakes in this region which produce crappies, sunnies, bass, walleyes, and northerns big enough to please any angler.

Sauk Centre is the birthplace of Sinclair Lewis, who made the town

Did you ever watch a raccoon fish? He's mostly after crayfish, and he does it by feel. His little hands work back and forth through the shallows and he gets a look of intense concentration on his face. Almost like a person trying to put a very small nut on a very small bolt on the hidden back side of a bulky machine, he looks this way and that with unfocused eyes, and I almost expect him to bite a lip or stick out the tip of his tongue as he zeros in on his invisible dinner. —L.B.

famous as the assumed setting of *Main Street*, the novel that shocked small towns across the United States. His boyhood home at 812 Sinclair Lewis Avenue (formerly Third Street) has been restored to its early-1900s appearance, and the Sinclair Lewis Museum is in the public library. Lewis won international acclaim as the first American to be awarded the Nobel Prize for literature. Before he died in 1951, he had written twenty-three novels including *Babbitt, Elmer Gantry,* and *Arrowsmith.*

On May 22, 1927, news flashed around the world that Charles A. Lindbergh, Jr. had successfully flown solo nonstop from New York to Paris, and the world had a hero. Everywhere, wild, joyous celebrations greeted the modest, unassuming young flier whose boyhood home was Little Falls, and Minnesota promptly claimed him as "her son." Shortly after his historic flight, what seemed like everyone in Minneapolis and Saint Paul, including my family, mobbed the old airport landing field to catch a glimpse of "Lucky Lindy" and his plane, "The Spirit of St. Louis." I remember my usually dignified mother frantically pulling me through the crowd so we could get a better look before he was whisked away in a limousine.

Young Charles spent winters in Washington, D.C. where his father was a Minnesota congressman, and summers at "the farm." The house, now the focal point of Charles A. Lindbergh State Park, south of Little Falls, has been restored and furnished to look as it did from 1907 to 1920. A duck pond that Charles built in 1919 has his name scratched in the concrete. When we walked down to the nearby stream, one of his favorite haunts, a beautiful brown mink flowed over and between the rocks in a leisurely departure. The interpretive center, on the bank of the Mississippi River, has exhibits that tell of three generations of Lindberghs, including the very distinguished career of Charles, Jr. after his famous flight.

Just about any vacation activity you can think of is available in the Brainerd area. It is in the midst of hundreds of lakes where some of Minnesota's most famous resorts are located. In Brainerd, An animated Paul Bunyan greets youngsters by name as they enter the amusement center, named for him, and the drone of car races at the Brainerd International Raceway can be heard throughout the summer. Antique shops and country stores draw browsers and shoppers to Crosslake at the entrance to the Whitefish chain of lakes. Wednesday afternoon turtle races are held in the charming community of Nisswa, which has easy access to Gull Lake. At Crosby, at the site of the original Croft Mine, visitors can experience a simulated four-hundred-foot drop into a deep-shaft mine on the Cuyuna Iron Range.

Cloudy days are not dull days during the fall color season. Sugar and red maples, oaks, aspens, birches, and shrubs all seem to glow with an inner light on sunless days. The absolute silence of this October morn seemed so right that I found myself holding my breath as I listened to the quiet. —L.B.

Common loon. —N.B.

A nice change of pace on an outdoor vacation is the chance to freshen up and to see a play. Summer theaters present popular titles near Bemidji, Brainerd, and Alexandria and in Fergus Falls.

On almost any northern Minnesota lake, a special sound captures our attention—a weird lonely cry, or a wild laughing call. These are the unmistakable calls of the common loon, Minnesota's state bird.

The streamlined loon, about the size of a goose, is sleek black and white, with a necklace of vertical black and white stripes and ruby red eyes. Because of its weight, it has to run on the water, splashing for some distance before it's airborne. On its sunset flights above the treetops, its tremulous call can be heard a long way. The loon is awkward on land, but a superb diver and swimmer, pursuing fish at great depths. Observing them dive and guessing where they will pop up again can be great fun. These symbols of our wilderness are protected by law and should never be molested.

The Mille Lacs Indian Museum, operated by the Minnesota Historical Society on the southwest shore of Lake Mille Lacs, is an excellent place to see how the Dakota (Sioux) and Ojibway (Chippewa) Indians lived, and to learn about the decisive and dramatic battle that drove the last Dakota from this area and about the effect of the fur trade on both tribes. Life-size dwellings in settings

If I'm away from Minnesota during the fall color season, I feel as if I've skipped a part of my life. So when I'm here, I try to be at all of the best places at once. That's difficult when it takes all day to drive about twenty miles, stopping every quarter mile to saturate my eyes, as well as film, with delicious color. This birch and maple forest is in the Tamarac National Wildlife Refuge. —L.B.

of the four seasons, and many artifacts, tools, and furnishings, show how the Indian was able to live with and from nature.

One time I watched two of the older women of the band doing beadwork explain the process. That night I tried my hand at it, and my failure only increased my admiration for their painstaking skill.

Maple sugar products and handcrafted items of birch bark and buckskin, made by the local Ojibway, are for sale, and sometimes traditional dances are performed at the Indian Community Center near the museum.

Excavations in Mille Lacs–Kathio State Park have unearthed artifacts made by prehistoric Indians who lived at Petaga Point between 3000 and 1000 B.C. Other excavations have shown significant habitation by other cultures. An interpretive center on Petaga Point focuses on the fascinating archaeology of this national historic landmark. There is an excellent trail system in this ten-thousand-acre park.

Few foods can tickle the taste buds so delightfully as the wild foods of Minnesota. Wild rice, growing in shallow lakes, has been a staple food of the Indians for centuries. To harvest it, they carefully tap the rice kernels into their canoes as they pole through rice beds. When Les was a boy, wild rice was breakfast cereal at his house. Now it's a gourmet treat for special occasions. Wild blueberries, strawberries, and raspberries, free for the picking, are far more flavorful than domestic varieties. Finding yourself in a good patch of wild berries can be sheer ecstasy.

For sportsmen and -women, Minnesota long has provided good hunting for deer, grouse, pheasant, and waterfowl. Fish, fresh from a cold-water lake and into the frying pan, is something to write home about. And something to take home as a gift, or to savor with your own pancakes, is pure maple syrup from a Minnesota sugar bush.

Whitetail deer live virtually everywhere within their range—forests, brushland, cornfields, cemeteries, suburbs, even in small wild places deep within cities. It seems that if the habitat is there—browse, cover, water, enough space to outmaneuver humans and dogs—the word gets around and a few whitetails move in. —L.B.

The South

The highway that follows the Mississippi River south from the Twin Cities has been called one of the most scenic drives in America. "Old Man River" has carved a wide and winding path, and the high bluffs on either side provide ever-changing panoramas and spectacular lookout points.

Leaving the Metro area at Hastings, the first river town south of the Twin Cities, we like to browse in the antique shops. We purchased a graceful cast-iron laundry stove with lovely bas-relief panels (patented 1865) that heats our home, from one shop, and a china cupboard that came from an Iowa farmstead, at another. The Le Duc Mansion, one of the finest examples of Victorian Gothic style in Minnesota, was built during the Civil War.

Wherever the state map displays the word "dam" and a heavy line across the Mississippi River, there are locks through which tugboats must push a line of huge barges. We never have ceased to marvel at the maneuvering ability of the pilots who steer the barges through the locks with what seems like only inches to spare. In Hastings, an observation tower at U.S. Lock and Dam Number 2 makes it possible to watch the boats and gigantic barges passing through.

Les and I like roaming back roads, and in the river country, almost any side road winds and dips from hilltop into draws and valleys. One such road goes down into the Cannon River Valley to secluded Welch, nestled between sandstone cliffs, then south to Vasa and back to the Mississippi at Red Wing. There is canoeing and tubing service on the Cannon in summer, and chalets for skiing in Welch in winter. The Cannon Valley Trail for hiking, biking, and cross-country skiing connects Cannon Falls, Welch, and Red Wing.

We have found Red Wing an exceptionally friendly city as well as beautiful. The restored Sheldon Theatre is called a "jewel box." Group tours can see *Echoes of Sheldon,* recounting its history from opening night in 1904. The restored Saint James Hotel, on the register for historic places, offers fine dining as do many other restaurants, and there are dinner cruises on an excursion boat.

The Memorial Park Scenic Skyline Drive climbs to the top of Sorin's Bluff overlooking the city and the river. Below Red Wing, the river widens to form thirty-five-mile-long Lake Pepin, famous for boating and fishing.

One of our favorite side trips is to Frontenac State Park and old Frontenac. The quiet settlement on the river is seemingly untouched by

Bluff after bluff, great ramparts confine the Mississippi River to its wild valley. Between the valley walls is an island and backwater wilderness hundreds of miles long. This broad band of wild land and water belongs to all of us, for much of it is a national wildlife refuge. —L.B.

the twentieth century, and that's the way the residents like it. In fact, Israel Garrard, who built Saint Hubert's Lodge as his home in 1856, gave land to the railroad west of town so that it wouldn't come through the village and disturb its tranquility. The Westerveldt House, built in 1854, is the oldest of several Greek Revival style homes built in the mid-nineteenth century. In the late 1800s, many famous Americans came by river steamer to vacation, paint, and hunt.

Frontenac State Park surrounds the village. There is an expansive view from the top of Point-No-Point and an Indian ceremonial rock four hundred feet above Lake Pepin. During spring bird migration, the park is an excellent birding place with chances to see some of the more unusual species such as blue-gray gnatcatcher, prothonotary warbler, and bald eagle.

Because rivers were Minnesota's first highways, river towns were the first to be established. Lake City, whose streets are lined with many fine old homes, is located at one of the most scenic spots on Lake Pepin. An excursion boat ride is a good way to enjoy some of that scenery. Water-skiing began here in 1922 on a pair of homemade skis. A block-long fishing pier is a convenient and good place to catch over ten varieties of fish including walleye and striped bass.

River country is apple orchard country. Many excellent varieties are grown, and signs to orchards greet travelers along the way. Some devotees make special autumn trips to purchase their favorite kind of apple, and to relish the rich color of the hardwood foliage as well.

When my mother graduated from high school in Wabasha in 1903, it was a busy river town. A presently famous establishment was famous back then, too. The Anderson Hotel, claimed to be Minnesota's oldest operating hotel, was built in 1856. Other historic buildings here and throughout the state have been preserved, many serving as bed-and-breakfast inns.

From November to March, an eagle observatory at the city deck on Lawrence Boulevard draws spectators who come to see wintering bald eagles. Our country's national emblem is making a comeback, and there's an unmistakable thrill to seeing one or several of these huge birds with an eighty-inch wingspan soaring over the river or perched in a tree. Eagles may be spotted at other points along the river, too.

Wabasha is at the northern boundary of the Upper Mississippi River Wildlife and Fish Refuge, which extends three hundred miles south. Timbered island backwaters and marshes are rich in animal and plant life. One early spring day we were thrilled to see thousands of white tundra swans on

It was a wonderful morning to be out—mild, calm, and sunny. Wisps of steam rose from the stream. The previous night's chill had dressed the willow branches in a fragile frost soon to be vanquished by the sun. —N.B.

Apple orchard. —C.B.

the river below a wayside lookout point near Weaver.

Whitewater State Park is a Shangri-la tucked away in a valley surrounded by unusual cliffs and limestone formations. Wild turkeys, reintroduced in the area, have multiplied so that a sighting of these shy birds is possible.

The landmark at Winona is Sugarloaf Bluff, rising like a sentinel high above the city. Another high vantage point, accessible by car, is Garvin Heights Park where travelers can see thirty miles in every direction. Fishing and boating on the river and the miles of backwaters, eating someone else's catch at the famous Hot Fish Shop, cruising the river on a paddle wheeler, viewing the roses at Lake Park—these are just some of the things to do in Winona.

Many homes and commercial buildings are of historic and architectural interest, especially the headquarters of Watkins Products, Incorporated. It was the world's largest private office building when it was built in 1912, with huge and intricate stained glass windows. Winona is known as the "stained glass capital of America" because of its many nationally known studios.

The drive west from Winona to Rochester is one of the loveliest in

Having turkey for Thanksgiving? Even though your bird may be from a farmer's all-white flock, it is a descendant of this bird's ancestors—in a roundabout way. Turkeys are native only to North and Central America. Early explorers took some turkeys, domesticated by Central American Indians, back to Europe with them. Immigrants brought them to America, and all of our modern domestic turkeys are relatives of those early travelers.

Though overshot to extinction on much of its original range, the wild turkey has been re-introduced in many states and again thrives as a game bird. —L.B.

Scarlet tanager. —L.B.

southeastern Minnesota, through rolling countryside. There is an old water-powered mill at Stockton.

Above the river road at Homer, the Bunnell House is of interest for its Gothic Revival design and details and for its historic significance. It was built in 1849 by the first permanent white residents of the county, and it is now open to the public.

At La Moille, we like to sidetrack over to Pickwick, a tiny crossroads center in an idyllic setting. Willows droop over the millpond, reflecting a four-story mill of cut stone. Here time does seem to have stood still.

At Dakota, we like to take County Road 12 that winds its way through a narrow canyon to the top of the bluffs, and then drive south on Apple Blossom Drive (County Road l) to see the Mississippi Valley from topside. Near La Crescent is a high point overlooking endless apple orchards on the slopes below and a view into Wisconsin and Iowa as well. The road then drops down through orchard after orchard. La Crescent and apples are synonymous. Over ten varieties are grown here and shipped all over the United States and Canada.

Les and I have often commented on how southeastern Minnesota seems to be a treasure of scenic beauty and recreational opportunities. The Root River country offers marvelous exploration, state parks for camping and

I had my camera set up by this forest-bordered waterfall in downtown Pickwick (See the old Pickwick mill through the trees in the background?), when a young fisherman entered the scene. As you know, I usually exclude people from my pictures, but this boy belongs here, as a deer would by a wilder pool. When he saw my big view camera mounted on the tripod, he politely asked if he would be in the way if he fished the pool. I told him

I was waiting for an overcast sky (clouds were building) so he could go ahead. I asked him his name, expecting Chuck or Tom or Butch. "Lance Michael Henderson" was his reply. Lance lives in Pickwick and has caught many a brooky in this pool. The cast on his arm was the result of a typical kid accident. He was climbing and grabbed the wrong thing, a loose concrete block. —L.B.

Beaver Creek. —C.B.

picnicking, trout streams and ponds, canoeing, swimming, golf—and caves. Evidence of good farming practice, necessary to prevent soil erosion, is everywhere, in wooded hillsides, contour plowing, grass runways, terracing, and strip farming.

Choice Beaver Creek Valley State Park is almost hidden between heavily wooded hills. A cold, fast-moving trout stream flows through the valley. We like searching out old mills, and the Old Schech Mill, built in 1876, stands near Sheldon north of Beaver Creek Park. It is the only water-powered mill still operating in Minnesota.

One town name we find curious is Money Creek, given to a little community north of Houston. Some say a gentleman crossing that creek, which flows through town, had his money tucked in his hat. The wind blew it off and his money got wet. He spread the bills on rocks to dry, but the pesky wind blew them back into the water, and they floated downstream out of his reach.

Driving west from Money Creek to Rushford, we like to go by way of Vinegar Hill (County Road 26 and then 27). I thought I smelled vinegar the first time we traveled this road that twists around the hill, but it was just my imagination. It was named by an early settler for a hill back in Illinois. But for

Valley farms in southeastern Minnesota are naturally beautiful. Large, square, flat fields may be easier to plough, but these curving strips of fertile land tucked into wooded hillsides create a landscape where man seems to fit more into the natural order of the world. —C.B.

a drive full of nice little surprises, this can't be beat. Valleys seem to branch off in every direction as the road climbs and dips past cliff gardens and into hollows. The Vinegar Hill road is just one of dozens of side roads we've explored and loved in this region.

Although we don't fish for trout, we have enjoyed visiting many of the private trout-rearing ponds in this section of the state. Some charge a fee for fishing, and some raise trout for restaurants, shipping the fish live. The State Fish Hatchery at Lanesboro offers some very interesting information about trout on its tours, and a chance to see some real lunkers in the brood pond.

On a hot summer day, one sure way to keep cool is to visit a cave where the temperature remains at forty-eight degrees. Niagara Cave, south of Harmony, was discovered in 1924 by two boys looking for lost pigs. What a discovery! Today a one-hour tour leads past odd-shaped formations into large chambers and onto a bridge overlooking a sixty-foot waterfall with a seventy-foot vaulted dome above it.

Harmony is near the largest Amish community in the state. Tours are available to visit farms to learn about a simple life style, and to purchase Amish crafts.

Forestville/Mystery Cave State Park, southwest of Preston, is a gem of historical interest and beauty. The original settlement of Forestville was a trading center and stagecoach stop between La Crosse and Mankato. Furs and produce were traded for flour and other supplies at Tom Meighan's store, established in 1853. Union soldiers drilled here during the Civil War. In the 1870s, the railroad bypassed Forestville and the town all but disappeared. In 1910, the door was locked on the Old Meighan Store of handpressed bricks and its contents. Today it's possible to browse the old store and learn a bit more of what life was like "back when." A network of park hiking trails leads to overlooks and a pioneer cemetery. Two creeks and the south fork of the Root River, known for good trout and smallmouth bass fishing, thread their way through the park.

Added to the park in 1988, Mystery Cave features twelve miles of underground routes carved out of the area's limestone and pitted dolomite. Turquoise Lake, a "pipe organ," "frozen" falls, and ribbon stalactites are some of the curious features. We have been told that southeastern Minnesota is honeycombed with caves, some as yet unmapped and perhaps still undiscovered—a challenge to spelunkers. Les joined a group of these cave explorers once, and his tale of straddling and jumping chasms, plus crawling through narrow openings, didn't tempt me to try it.

Forestville Store, Forestville/Mystery Cave State Park, is yesteryear for real. The shelves are still stocked with the quaint merchandise of grandfather's time. And there is nothing in the surrounding forest to jar you back to the present. The entire park is a lovely setting of streams, ravines, and valleys, little changed by the years since the store was built of handmade bricks in 1854. —L.B.

Canada geese landing at Silver Lake. —C.B.

Perhaps no Minnesota city is better known worldwide than Rochester. And probably no Minnesota city constantly attracts people from so many countries, all because of the Mayo Clinic, the renowned medical center founded by Dr. William W. Mayo and his sons in the late 1800s. Tours of the Mayo Clinic and Mayo Medical Museum are mind-boggling. Mayowood, the mansion of Drs. C. W. and C. H. Mayo, and the Plummer House are also open for tours.

On Silver Lake, within the city limits, as many as thirty-three thousand Canada geese spend at least part of the winter on the water, warmed by the power plant. A few hundred stay in the summer, too. While the geese are tame enough to be hand fed at Silver Lake, they become wild once they fly outside the city. Few sights are as thrilling as a flock of geese coming in for a landing, and at Silver Lake the thrill can be repeated ad infinitum. Fine restaurants and a wide selection of entertainment and recreational facilities make this cosmopolitan city ready for company all year around.

Around Rochester, roads lead in every direction to interesting and scenic spots. Many rivers such as the Root, with outfitters at Lanesboro, Rushford, and Chatfield, are ideal for novice canoeing except during high

Before the coming of agriculture, southern Minnesota was covered with a rich mixture of forest and prairie. Both gave way to the plow to help feed a hungry world. Today, remnants of both prairie and forest are treasured as rare bits of natural beauty, and many are preserved in state parks, Nature Conservancy holdings, or as nature centers. This lovely stream flows through the Jay C. Hormel Nature Center at Austin. —L.B.

A "nice ol' barn." —L.B.

water. State parks have hiking, biking, and cross-country ski trails. Some abandoned railroad lines have been converted to these uses also.

Mantorville is a charming town that has consciously preserved its 1860s appearance ever since a restoration movement inspired by Irene Felker began in the 1970s. A cut limestone hotel built in 1857, known as the Hubbell House, was a popular stagecoach stop. Today it is a fine restaurant. The stone courthouse, built in 1871; the old Opera House; the newspaper office; the Congregational church; and the old Episcopal church, now the Dodge County Historical Museum, are all accent pieces in this town where almost every home and building fits the restoration theme. Let's hope more towns follow Mantorville's example before precious landmarks disappear.

Compared with the time when it was larger than Rochester, the community of Wasioja, northwest of Mantorville, is now almost a ghost town. Once on a territorial stagecoach route, it boasted a fairground, racetrack, limestone slab sidewalks, and a newspaper. When the railroad bypassed the town, all these disappeared, but some landmarks remain. The old stage hotel is now a home. The Baptist church is believed to be the oldest of its denomination in the state. A huge rock in the yard of the stone

Have you ever felt very close to history? I did at this beautiful old stagecoach stop in southeastern Minnesota. I could picture the driver and guard climbing down to help passengers. This sturdy inn is a remnant of the period when stagecoach routes crisscrossed the land before the coming of railroads. Now it rests quietly beside a seldom-used country lane. —L.B.

schoolhouse wore out plenty of pants and shoes when used as a slide. At the southeast edge of town, almost hidden in a spruce grove, stands the lonely skeleton of Wasioja Seminary. When recruits for the Civil War were called for, ninety of the students marched to the stone recruiting station (built for a bank and still there) to enlist. That closed the school. It burned in 1905 leaving its stark remains.

Mention Northfield, and Jesse James comes to mind. James, the notorious bank bandit, raided the Northfield Bank in 1876. But Northfield also is a peaceful college town on the Cannon River with two beautiful campuses. At Saint Olaf, the highlight of the year is the Christmas concert season. Tickets are hard to come by, but we were lucky to be guests of friends one year to hear the famous choirs and orchestra, following a sumptuous smorgasbord at the college which included my first taste of lutefisk, that famous Scandinavian delicacy. At Carleton College, on the other side of town, the May Fete is an annual event.

If time allows, we take the scenic route between Northfield and Faribault via Nerstrand Woods State Park. Here is a remnant of the "Big Woods" of oak and maples that once stretched from the Mississippi River to Mankato, sheltering Indian villages and pioneer settlements.

Faribault was founded by Alexander Faribault whose frame house built in 1853 still stands at 12 Northeast First Avenue. Bishop Henry B. Whipple, who was a nationally recognized champion and friend of the Indians in the mid-1800s, established three well-known schools in Faribault: Shattuck Military Academy, Saint Mary's Hall, and Saint James School for Boys. The Peony Farm in June, Chrysanthemum Gardens in September, great caves for curing blue cheese, and the Faribo Woolen Mills are some of the attractions that draw thousands of visitors to Faribault.

The southwestern section of Minnesota isn't usually considered tourist country, but Les and I have found travel here very interesting. There are numerous reminders of dramatic events that shaped pioneer life in Minnesota, many of them from the summer of 1862 when the Dakota (Sioux) Indians waged war to drive the white settlers from the Minnesota River Valley. Prosperous farms and modern cities now cover the land, but searching out visual evidence of our past adds a special purpose to a trip through this lush green countryside dotted with blue lakes.

It was almost beyond our comprehension as we stood in quiet, secluded Traverse des Sioux park, two miles north of Saint Peter, to imagine eight thousand Dakota gathered on this site. They had come in July 1851, setting

November. The bright colors of fall have faded; summer birds have migrated; there's not enough snow yet for winter sports. So most folks stay home. Drab? I'd rather say that November is subdued, restrained, quiet. Empty? No, full!—of wildness, cleanness, brisk, invigorating air. A November day like this is one I'd unselfishly like to share with lots of kindred spirits—about a mile apart. —L.B.

Minneopa Falls State Park, Mankato. —L.B.

The common name "white trout lily" refers to the mottled leaves of this spring wildflower of the hardwoods, which resemble the markings of trout. The flowers last but a few days, but the wonderful foliage adds interest to the forest floor throughout the summer. —C.B.

up tipis in tiers around a central treaty ground, to negotiate with representatives of the U.S. Government. Here and at Mendota on Pilot Knob, the Dakota signed treaties ceding nearly twenty-four million acres in the Minnesota Territory, as well as in Iowa and Dakota, for less than eight cents an acre. Within a few months the land boom was on, and white settlers rushed in to establish farms and villages along the length of the Minnesota River.

Dissatisfaction over terms of treaties, failure of the U.S. government to fulfill treaty obligations (including annuity payments and promises of food), forced acculturation to Euro-American ways, and starvation are some of the reasons given for the Dakota War of 1862.

Minneopa Falls in Minneopa State Park at Mankato is almost a sister to Minnehaha Falls in appearance, tumbling into a deep, rocky, and wooded gorge. The Blue Earth and Minnesota rivers meet in the park. An interesting, old stone windmill has been restored here. Prairie flowers abound in the area adjacent to the campgrounds. Les and I once spent a beautiful morning there photographing blazing stars in full bloom.

The scene was quite different in 1701. The previous fall Pierre Le Sueur and a crew of Frenchmen struggled up the Mississippi in two canoes and a sailboat to this point, expecting to find a bonanza in copper ore. After building the valley's first fort, and consuming four hundred buffalo during the winter, they dug thirty thousand pounds of earth, and Le Sueur took four thousand pounds of the best "copper ore" back to France, only to learn the blue clay was worthless.

One year, Les and I made a special trip to Jeffers Petroglyphs as a way to celebrate my birthday. Hearing about the rock carvings done by hunting peoples as long as five thousand years ago, I had to see them. We drove the county road west from Comfrey and turned south on County Road 2 for a mile to the entrance. What appears to be a rather low, treeless ridge holds secrets of the past yet to be revealed. No one knows for sure who the people were who pecked at the red rock outcroppings, leaving crude but recognizable pictures of bison, bear, wolf, turtle, and elk, as well as human stick figures, some holding atlatls, a spear-throwing device used to increase the power of the human arm. Many other glyphs added to our feeling of awe.

On the north side of the Minnesota River, between Fort Ridgely State Park and New Ulm on County Highway 21, is the old Harkin General Store returned to its 1870s appearance by the Minnesota Historical Society. Les and I met the granddaughter of the original owner several years ago when she graciously showed us the curious items left in the store at the time it closed

This photograph shows but a small sampling of the many animals, weapons, and symbols chipped into the rock at Jeffers Petroglyphs. The figures have been varnished to make them clearly visible. —C.B.

in 1901.

New Ulm has lots of personality, history, and oompah-pah. Its broad streets and beautiful parks were planned in every detail by Christian Prignitz, one of the German immigrants who settled here in 1855. The city retains and nourishes its German heritage, evident in the special events such as the Polka Festival when the streets bounce with happy rhythms of its many dance bands; organizations like the Turnverein for physical fitness and the New Ulm Battery, a civilian military unit; the architecture of the old post office and a picturesque brewery; and Hermann—a statue high above the city, standing with his sword held skyward. Les teases me about Hermann who is one of my heroes, but I consider him worthy of veneration. Hermann was a great German warrior who led his tribes in battle to end the oppressive rule of the Romans over his people two thousand years ago. Hermann Lodges of the U.S. erected this huge monument in his memory. A climb up the stairs of the monument gives a great view of the city.

New Ulm suffered heavy losses in the Dakota War of 1862 when almost two hundred buildings were destroyed. Three that survived can be seen today: the Kiesling House at 220 North Minnesota Street, the only surviving home of the conflict; the Erd Building, now a restaurant at 108 North Minnesota Street, where settlers took refuge in the basement with a keg of powder intending to destroy themselves if the Indians took the settlement; and the Forster Building, 117 North Broadway, where bullet holes are still visible on the north wall. The Brown County Historical Society Museum in the Old Post Office at Center and Broadway has more information about the Indian War.

Monuments commemorating events of the war are scattered throughout southwestern Minnesota, testimony to lives lost in that bitter conflict.

Fort Snelling was never attacked, but Fort Ridgely, now a state park on the upper Minnesota River off Minnesota Highway 4, was the scene of two of the fiercest battles of the Dakota War of 1862. Walking over the ground of the fort today, the story of bravery and heroism on both sides unfolds in dramatic fashion.

The fort, built in 1853 to protect white settlers, was merely a group of buildings without a stockade, vulnerable from three ravines. Three hundred settlers had streamed into the fort on August 18 and 19 for safety, complicating its defense. If the Dakota had attacked then, the fort would have been defended by only a handful of soldiers led by a nineteen-year-old lieutenant who had the mumps. Captain Marsh, the post commander, had left with a company of forty soldiers to aid the settlers at the Lower Sioux Agency who had been

Friends from Saint Peter, Minnesota, showed us this lovely group of white lady's slippers not too far from their home. The blossoms certainly look like delicate slippers, graceful and petite. —N.B.

attacked that morning. He lost his life with twenty-four of his men when ambushed by the Dakota at the Redwood Ferry.

By the time of the first attack by four hundred Indians on Fort Ridgely on August 20, the fort's defense had increased from twenty-nine to almost 180 men. Two days later, an estimated eight hundred Indians attacked the fort. A well-drilled crew, manning the post's few cannons, is credited with driving off the Indians.

Today the stone commissary has been rebuilt and the log powder magazine restored. Archaeological excavations have uncovered foundations of other buildings, and artifacts and a film reveal much about the fort and its occupants.

The Lower Sioux Agency, southeast of Morton on County Road 2, was built in 1853 as an administration center for the first Dakota reservation, established by the treaties of Traverse des Sioux and Mendota. It resembled a small village with stores, shops, mills, dozens of homes, and a stone warehouse. Eight years of pressure by the government, traders, and white settlers on the Dakota people climaxed in their rebellion.

At sunrise on August 18, 1862, Dakota warriors staged a surprise attack, killing twenty white people and burning and looting the buildings. Upper Sioux Agency buildings were also sacked and burned. Battles at New Ulm, Fort Ridgely, Birch Coulee, and Acton followed before the Indians were finally defeated at Wood Lake. On September 26, 269 white and mixed-bloods captured by Dakota were freed at Camp Release near present-day Montevideo. Nearly two thousand Dakota were tried in the weeks that followed, and 303 were sentenced to death. President Lincoln lowered the number, and thirty-eight were hanged at Mankato on December 26, a sad moment in a sorry period of American history.

An interpretive center at the Lower Agency has exhibits depicting the history of the eastern Dakota Indians from 1800 to the present.

Parks, bluffs, and gorges make Redwood Falls an especially beautiful city. Steamboats once unloaded supplies on the Minnesota River, and the cargo was carried from here by oxcart to North Dakota. The town had a gold rush in 1894, but after a year of digging up buckets of shiny quartz, the prospectors left and the promoters disappeared. But a real "gold mine" started in 1886. An enterprising young depot agent named Dick Sears notified other agents that he had unclaimed watches for sale. The mail orders netted him five hundred dollars, and that was the birth of Sears Roebuck and Company. Redwood Falls still encourages ingenuity, hosting an Inventors' Congress each year in June.

The grasslands of southern Minnesota can seem empty when viewed from afar, but close in there is an intricate, delicate beauty. —C.B.

One gentleman who pops up repeatedly in the stories of early events in Minnesota is Joseph R. Brown, another of my "heroes." I wish we could have known him for he seems to have been in on the beginning of things when people of action and foresight were needed. Starting as a drummer boy at Fort Snelling in 1819 while the fort was being built, he went on to be a soldier, fur trader, lumberman, founder of cities, legislator, editor, Indian agent, and inventor. Sinclair Lewis once said, "Perhaps as much as anyone, he was the inventor of the automobile."

He brought his wife, Susan, of French, Scottish, and Dakota blood, and their twelve children to live in a nineteen-room granite mansion on a slope overlooking the Minnesota River beyond the white settlements. Elegantly furnished (two grand pianos, crystal chandeliers, and damask drapes), it was the center of hospitality in the late 1850s. In 1862, while Mr. Brown was in New York to see about his inventions, the Dakota War broke out, and his wife and children were captured and the home was burned. Because Mrs. Brown could speak the Indians' language, she and the children were held captive but unharmed until their release at the end of the war. Remnants of the walls and a plaque showing how the original house probably looked are located on County Road 9 south of Sacred Heart.

In the Granite Falls vicinity, along U.S. Route 212, is some of the oldest rock on the crust of the earth, probably 3.7 billion years old, close in age to our planet itself. It was exposed by the erosive action of the ancient River Warren, which flowed from melting glaciers ten thousand years ago, and by highway construction.

During spring and fall migration periods, serious birders and people who merely enjoy the sight of birds gather at well-used flyways. One spring Les and I joined a group of birders in the Salt Lake area near the South Dakota border to welcome flocks of cormorants, white pelicans, geese, and smaller birds as they arrived from the South. It's a dead heart that doesn't quicken its beat at seeing skeins of geese shifting positions as they come closer, calling to each other in muted tones, then circling and dropping in on a Minnesota lake for the first time that year. What a marvelous phenomenon, migration.

On a night walk we heard snipes, their tail feathers whistling in aerial courting flights, and owls hooting in the woods.

The Lac qui Parle, Marsh, and Big Stone Lake reservoirs are all great birding and scenic areas. The western grebe, famous for its curious mating rituals and spectacular dancing, and the short-eared owl can sometimes be seen here. Potholes in the prairie are good places to see shorebirds not common in

I had spent the early morning photographing courtship rituals of western grebes, enthralled by the pairs of birds running in tandem over the water by my blind. Then the action turned to nest building, and I trained my camera on this grebe bringing a cattail blade to its floating nest that was anchored to other cattails. —c.b.

Prairie fire at Big Stone National Wildlife Refuge. —c.b.

other parts of Minnesota, such as the Wilson's phalarope that spins like a top in the water to stir up its prey, avocet, little blue heron, yellow-crowned night heron, and snowy and cattle egrets.

Northwest of Montevideo on Chippewa County Highway 13, off U.S. Highway 59, is the intriguing historic site of Lac qui Parle Mission. Joseph Renville, son of a French fur trader and Dakota mother, was an expedition guide for Zebulon Pike in 1805, then a captain on the British side in the War of 1812, before coming here to trade with the Indians about 1822. With servants and bodyguards Renville lived "in splendor quite like an African king" with his Indian wife. He invited missionaries to establish a Protestant mission and often participated in services himself. Here missionaries began translation of the Bible into the Dakota language, and Indians were taught agriculture and weaving of cloth. A replica of the mission chapel on the original site is a museum of Indian artifacts, pioneer relics, and exhibits on the development of the Dakota alphabet.

One year, we timed a visit to Pipestone National Monument to coincide with a performance of "The Song of Hiawatha" pageant. It is given on the last two weekends of July and the first one in August at the edge of the monument. Sitting in the natural amphitheater, watching the legend made famous by poet

The spring flowers of the woodlands may be but distant memories in August, but cone flowers, blazing stars, asters, and countless other prairie splendors are at their peak—right now! This prairie in Big Stone National Wildlife Refuge near Ortonville is one of the few remaining in Minnesota. —c.b.

Pipestone pipe. —L.B.

Henry Wadsworth Longfellow come alive on the shore of Lake Winona was a beautiful and memorable experience.

The Pipestone Quarry is one of the best known American Indian sites. For centuries, Indians have come here to get the red stone for their ceremonial pipes and figures. Many legends relate to the area and the stone, some romanticized and some authentic, but there is no doubt that the pipe was smoked in sacred rituals by many tribes. Few white people knew of the quarry until the noted artist of Indian life, George Catlin, came from New York in 1836 to sketch and to secure samples of the stone. In his honor the pipestone was named catlinite. Two years later, the U.S. government sponsored an exploring expedition of five men led by Joseph Nicollet. Their carved initials can be seen on Inscription Rock. In his report Nicollet mentioned three huge boulders called the Three Maidens. He told of Indians placing offerings in front of them before digging at the quarry.

A circle trail goes by part of the quarry. Les and I watched in fascination one evening as an Indian aimed his blows at just the right places to split huge chunks of the red rock. Only Indians are allowed to quarry the stone.

There are many points of interest along the trail such as Leaping Rock, a stone column twenty-three feet high, separated from surrounding ledges.

In early September the prairie dresses in colors more subtle than the gaudy northern hardwood forest's. Here in Pipestone National Monument dawn's soft light was just right for the landscape. —N.B.

Winnewissa Falls in Pipestone National Monument. —C.B.

Leaping to this rock and not losing one's balance was considered a feat to boast about. John C. Fremont, a member of Joseph Nicollet's 1838 expedition, successfully made this leap.

The trail winds up and down along lichen-covered rock cliffs, past delicate Winnewissa Falls and out onto the prairie. Just the variety of plantlife and flowers makes walking the trails an adventure. The museum has exhibits on the quarry and its legends, and pipestone items made by the Indians are for sale.

Fans of the Laura Ingalls Wilder books which inspired the television series, "Little House on the Prairie," may want to make a "pilgrimage" to Walnut Grove. The author grew up nearby, at first in a sod dugout on the banks of Plum Creek in the 1870s. The site is off County Road 5. There is a museum and tourist center in town, and a Pioneer Festival featuring a Wilder pageant, "Fragments of a Dream," is a July event.

Here's something to write home about. Twenty miles east of Walnut Grove, there's a chance to see or stay in an 1880s sod house at Sanborn. This kind of home was built by pioneers, using blocks of virgin prairie when there were no trees available.

South of Pipestone, near Blue Mounds State Park, lives one of my favorite

Colorful, and almost glazed in texture, Sioux quartzite cliffs rise above the trails at Pipestone National Monument. —C.B.

Bison bull, Blue Mounds State Park. —C.B.

authors, Frederick Manfred. Some of his novels are based on Indian legends or stories of early frontier life such as *Lord Grizzly* and *Conquering Horse;* others seem to grow from the soil of his beloved "Siouxland." *Scarlet Plume* is a tale of the Dakota War of 1862 in southwestern Minnesota.

Manfred's unusual former home, built against a rock cliff, is the visitor's center in Blue Mounds State Park. From a distance what looks like a bluish rock mound, rising from the prairie along the eastern edge of the park, becomes red at closer range. Legend has it that Indians once drove bison off the cliff to their deaths, but rather than heaps of buffalo bones, archaeologists have found tools and spearheads of long-ago nomadic cultures.

A remnant herd of bison grazing on prairie grass; 225 species of birds, some rare in Minnesota, such as the blue grosbeak; prickly pear cactus, an oddity in Minnesota; and one of the best examples of natural prairie—all combine to make this park a real treasure. There are trails, a swimming beach, and camping and picnicking grounds.

I think that Blue Mounds is a good place to bid farewell to you readers who have been with me and Les on this journey through our state. It has been a chance to take you along to some of the special places that we hoped you would enjoy. There's more to see and do in Minnesota, so don't stop here. Keep exploring!

Beyond the white darkness . . . ? Yesterday there were farms in the distance below this prairie bluff at Blue Mounds State Park. But this morning the wild prairie continues to the invisible horizon at the edge of the world. Bison bulls rumble their statements of invincibility back over the hill to the left. (They really do. There is a herd here grazing on the prairie grasses.) So maybe when the fog lifts, a circle of tipis will be a Sioux campground below—at least until the air is clear enough to discern them once again as farm buildings. —L.B.

Index

For more information about sites mentioned in this book, contact one of these organizations:

Minnesota Office of Tourism
375 Jackson Street, 250 Skyway Level
St. Paul, MN 55101
612-296-5029 ★ 800-652-9747 (in Minnesota) ★ 800-328-1461 (outside Minnesota)

Department of Natural Resources Information Center
500 Lafayette Road
St. Paul, MN 55155-4040
612-296-4776 (in the Twin Cities) ★ 800-652-9747, ask for DNR (in Minnesota) ★ 612-296-5484 (Telecommunications Device for Deaf)

Other Books by the Blacklocks

Ain't Nature Grand

published by Voyageur Press

Black Hills / Badlands: The Web of the West

published by Voyageur Press

Border Country, The Quetico-Superior Wilderness

published by Northword Press

The Geese of Silver Lake

published by Voyageur Press

Hidden Forest

published by Voyageur Press

Journeys to Door County

published by Voyageur Press

Meet My Psychiatrist

published by Voyageur Press

Minnesota Wild

published by Voyageur Press

Photographing Wildflowers: Techniques for the Advanced Amateur and Professional

published by Voyageur Press